Call to Arms

Call to Arms

A history of Military Communications
from the Crimean War to the Present Day

Focus Publishing

Call to Arms

Editors: Maureen Bridge
                        John Pegg

Jacket Design: Chris Lewis Associates
                        41 Charterhouse Square, London EC1M 6EA

Design: Heards Illustration and Graphic Design
                        Walreddon, Tavistock PL19 9EQ

Typesetting: Poster and Display Artists Limited
                        1 Parliament Terrace, Upper Parliament Street, Nottingham
                        NG1 5FX

Published by Focus Publishing at 4 Watts Road, Tavistock, Devon, PL19 8LF in association with BT Defence

Telephone: 01822 612987
© 2001 ISBN: 0-953 9809-0-1

Printed in the United Kingdom

CONTENTS

FOREWORD

by Peter Cochrane

One of the most redeeming features of our species is that we are often at our best when things are at their worst. Our history sees us rally and co-operate so that good overcomes evil and prosperity and peace can spring from adversity and war. From the earliest of times hunting for food and seeking to protect our offspring, families and tribe encouraged a rapid growth in our brainpower. The advantages of being able to throw projectiles accurately and create tools for the efficient procurement and preparation of meat and other foods, and most of all the ability to communicate, has effectively promoted us beyond all others. For sure our species would have achieved little without developing the ability to communicate complex ideas, concepts, situations and messages. And certainly we would not have come so far so fast without the artificial ability to communicate efficiently at a distance.

Telecommunications has changed, and continues to change, the course of human affairs in a manner and at a pace that is invisible to, and misunderstood by, most. For modern societies telecommunication networks are now the nervous system by which everything is organised and controlled. Without these networks we could not support the near six billion people on the planet, and our very civilisation would collapse. As a force for good, telecommunications has probably contributed more to preventing World War Three than any other factor, whilst as a force for evil it actively promotes the cause of the terrorist.

Modern military telecommunications now hold the vital cards in the deadly arena of war. Without accurate and timely information, and the immediate ability to communicate to and from distant mobile and fixed platforms, war can no longer be waged effectively. It should come as no surprise therefore that some of the biggest surges in the development of the base technologies of telecommunication have come about through the needs of war – both hot and cold. To be specific; the need for mobile communication during World War Two, followed by the Cold War, and the space race, created the competitive environment that led to all the base technologies we enjoy today. The transistor and the integrated circuit were no accident of alchemy – they were born out of a need for effective, efficient, reliable and low cost communication.

If Napoleon and his generals had been equipped with mobile phones then the outcome at Waterloo could have been quite different! But perhaps like the generals of World War One, they may not have appreciated the significance of timely information. The decisions of society, industry and military machines are made with and by people who have not always recognised the significance of new technologies. Often they have appeared as dinosaurs, not realising that the pain at the extremities of their ten-metre tails was in fact a significant input for survival. But once realised and the need recognised, they have invested heavily to correct any misapprehension.

No single book could hope to chart the entire history of warfare, or indeed just the one small corner concerned with military telecommunications. The subject is now vast, with a history encompassing every nation and spanning millennia. So this book is delightfully focussed in describing the British experience from Roman times to the present day. But more specifically it is concerned with the developments leading up to and including electronic communication, and in particular, the relationship with my own industrial organisation BT – or as it was once known – the GPO.

For me the historical perspective is always relevant and interesting, and in this volume you will find a wealth of references spanning the use of runners, beacons, wire line, optical fibre, radio, satellite, secret codes and encryption. Set in the context of land, sea and air warfare, another interesting facet is the difference between peace and wartime operations. The ability to condense development and deployment times when faced with a real crisis has to raise questions of cost effectiveness and efficiency as we are now in the 21st Century. If Internet time is now measured in dog years, then why not military technology development times also? There is ample evidence in these pages to suggest that we now know enough not to repeat the mistakes of past generations.

Given the vain hope that our species will at some time grow up and stop the senseless slaughter founded on religious, ethnic and territorial disputes, the overall theme of this book is both interesting and positive. For me there is only one disturbing feature; the number of people and technologies cited that I have been connected and worked with is far higher than I could have anticipated. I never expected to be a part of history so soon. Enjoy the read – I did.

Until December 2000, Peter Cochrane was BT's Head of Research and Technology.

Ancient Greek soldiers communicated with fire signals using beacons and coded torches for letters of the alphabet. They also had water telegraph devices, as illustrated, and sent messages using sunlight reflected on polished shields – the origin of the heliograph

INTRODUCTION

Good communication helps to win battles. This is as true now as it was in the days of the ancient Greeks. Until recent times, one of the greatest problems faced by any commander was how to transmit orders to troops and receive back accurate information about the state of the conflict.

Given a good vantage point, it was not usually difficult to control the opening stages of a battle. Keeping control was rather different. Even when he could see what action was needed, his orders might go astray or not arrive at all. If they arrived, the meaning might be misunderstood. The disastrous Charge of the Light Brigade during the Crimean War was the result of a badly written message.

On the other hand, good methods of communication must have existed before the first Roman invasion of Britain, for by the time the invaders arrived, the Ancient Britons had mustered some 60,000 defenders. There must also have been satisfactory communication in the other direction because the Romans equipped their ships with artillery to break up any concentrations of defenders on the beaches. Spies must have existed on both sides even then. Nothing is new; we have just got smarter and faster.

The earliest form of long distance signalling was the man running on foot carrying a written or verbal message. The most famous foot messenger was Pheidippedes who, in 490BC, carried the news of victory at the Battle of Marathon the 26 miles to Athens and then dropped dead! Long distance foot races are named after this feat. Runners or men on horseback were used to carry messages for many centuries. Sometimes, when he brought bad news, the messenger could be killed as a reward for his efforts.

During the Peninsular War – 1804-1814 – the Duke of Wellington became the first Commander to organise a regular mounted messenger service. Horse messages continued to be used on the battlefield until the end of World War One. The tradition of the mounted messenger was continued with motorcycle despatch riders into the 20th Century.

In the 1st Century BC, the Persian King, Darius, set up a chain of soldiers on hill tops to shout messages to each other. It is claimed that signals could travel 450 miles in 48 hours using this method. The military use of drums for signalling on the battlefield continued until the end of the 19th Century. Trumpets have also been used since ancient times. In army camps around the world trumpets and bugles are still used to mark certain times of day and to convey orders. The disadvantage of sound signals is their limited range, competing noise and the fact that sound travels more slowly than light.

The Greeks experimented with fire signals and the use of reflected sunlight on polished shields (heliograph). According to the Greek writer Aeschylus, Agamemnon had devised a means of communication over distance in 1084BC when he managed to convey the news of the fall of Troy to his queen Clytemnestra. The watchman had been waiting ten years for the message which arrived by a line of beacons.

The Greek historian Polybius writing in the 2nd Century BC described a method using ten torches divided into two groups of five. The Greek alphabet has fewer letters than ours and does not line up precisely with those adopted in modern western languages, but the principle was as follows:

	i	ii	iii	iv	v
i	A	B	C	D	E
ii	F	G	H	IJ	K
iii	L	M	N	O	P
iv	Q	R	S	T	U
v	V	W	X	Y	Z

The number of torches displayed by the first group shows the line and the second group the letter.

The Roman Army used lights and signal towers. They also used a programme of smoke signals; there was a network of signal stations in the Roman Empire and the army used them regularly.

The fire and smoke system was practised in the Middle Ages. By day smoke signals were sent from signal towers; by night the smoke signals were replaced by pillars of flame. The approach of the Spanish Armada in 1588 was signalled by lighting a chain of beacons from the West Country to London, although this could only convey a simple warning. Flags or banners can only be seen during daylight over a short distance. Not until the early 19th Century was the language (protocol) agreed for flag signalling.

The North American Indians perfected smoke signalling. Not only did they use a varying number of puffs but by throwing substances on the fire they changed the colours of the smoke. Even in the 1914-18 war rockets with yellow, green, brown or purple puffs of smoke were used as recognition signals and had the advantage of defying imitation.

North American Native Indians were not the first to use coloured smoke signals; this form of communication was a Roman invention. The Indians perfected this, however, by throwing substances on the fire which produced more varied colours, giving the ability to convey more complex messages

All methods of visual signalling of course are easily open to error both in sending and being read. An example in classical literature is the story of Aegeus and Theseus. Theseus set out to slay the Minotaur. If successful it was agreed that he would change the colour of his sails from black to white for the return journey. He forgot to do so. His father Aegeus seeing the black sails thought he was dead and cast himself into the sea and drowned. This could be the first documented example of a 'communications cock-up'!

In 1684 Dr Robert Hook published a Royal Society paper called *How to communicate one's mind at distances in as short a time almost as a man can write what he would have sent*. He proposed the use of simple shapes hung in a wooden frame, to represent the letters of the alphabet. Experiments were carried out as early as 1672 between Arundel House and a boat moored in the Thames half a mile away. This was an early precursor of the Shutter Telegraph. The word telegraph means literally "write (or describe) at a distance".

Nearly one hundred years later, in 1779, Vice Admiral Lord Shuldham established a signals code which was to be used from the tower of Maker Church, Plymouth at the time of the Franco-Spanish invasion scare. The signals code used pennants, flags and balls in specific combinations to convey a range of messages.

Both Dr Hook and Vice Admiral Lord Shuldham, in their different ways, pointed the way to military communications in the 19th Century – which is where this book begins.

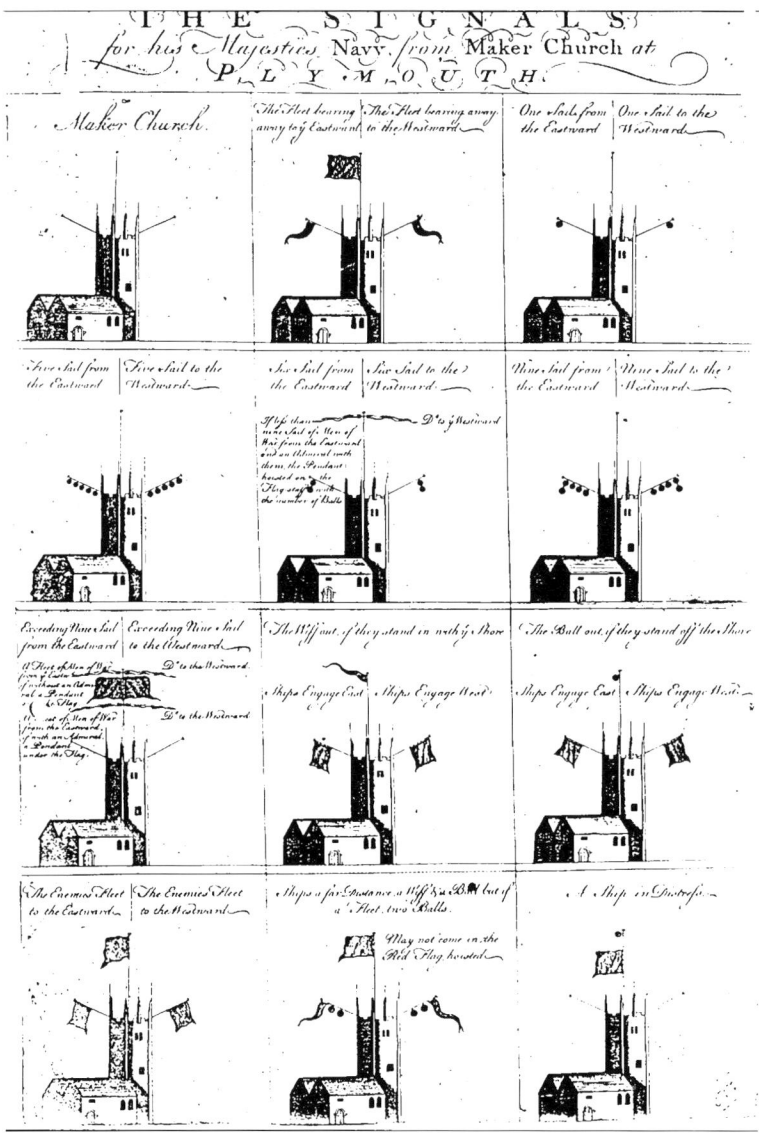

In 1779, Vice Admiral Lord Shuldham established a signals code designed to be used from the tower of Maker Church, Plymouth, during a Franco-Spanish invasion scare. It involved a variety of pennants, flags and balls, used in specific combinations to convey a range of messages. France and Spain were still hostile to Britain following the loss of their American possessions during the Seven Years War, 1756-1763

THE 19TH CENTURY: FROM THE SHUTTER TELEGRAPH TO THE CRIMEA

Simon John Piggott

Aged 30, Simon John Piggott had served with Nelson's Flagship at Trafalgar. He wore a pigtail and after returning home had married Jane Treleven, a Plymouth girl.

Simon could write simple English, was a god-fearing Methodist and had taken the Pledge. His drawback to the Navy was his ankle; injured at Trafalgar, he could only run with a limp but he played down his disability.

He was quietly proud of his post as one of two foremastmen or jack-tars to the Number 4 Shutter Telegraph Station at Devonport. The year was 1808 and the Shutter was said to be the thing of the future.

The full complement of a main shutter station was an officer, a midshipman and one or two men. The station itself was usually a hut with a high-pitched roof and a smaller lean-to outhouse. The shutter frame was supported by struts which were secured to the eaves.

At Devonport, he worked the ropes under Lieutenant Dudley Holmes, Royal Navy, whose responsibility it was to write down the messages. Midshipman Tony Bligh stood at the telescope.

The Navy List of the time showed that lieutenants on Coast Signals Stations received 7s 6d a day plus half-pay for their rank. Midshipmen got 2s a day plus half-pay of a fourth rate. Simon got 2s a day plus his lodgings, coal and free candles.

Between Plymouth and London there were 22 stations. Weather permitting, it was possible to send a message in minutes between any of these stations and this was a remarkable achievement considering that, if sent by post-horse, the average speed of transmission would not have exceeded 12 miles an hour – no faster than in Roman times.

Tests of the new line showed that in good weather Simon could get a simple message to London in 12 minutes, and on a clear day, Plymouth could receive a signal from the Capital in about 20 minutes.

The 'Shutter Telegraph', a signalling system designed by the Reverend Lord George Murray in 1796, was based on an earlier French invention. A series of shutters spelled out words letter by letter, and a message could be transmitted from London to Portsmouth in 15 minutes or less; the Shutter Relay Station built at Blandford Racecourse 1806-25 is shown above

The conflict with revolutionary France which began in 1793 was a new kind of war. Huge armies moved over the vast plains of central Europe, so good communications were essential. In 1792, a Frenchman, Claude Chappe, invented his Radiated Telegraph machine, a form of visual signalling using pivoted arms to send signals along the roads which radiated from Paris. It looked not unlike a windmill and the message symbol was carried on an extended arm. The message was not spelt out but was given in code which the reader then had to look up in a dictionary.

Chappe's invention also aroused interest in Britain where the Admiralty in London was looking for a means of communicating with its naval bases. Only four years after Chappe's invention, a system designed by the Revd Lord George Murray, similar in form to Chappe's invention, was eventually adopted. It used six shutters in a frame 30 feet high by 20 feet wide (9m x 6m) and used letters to spell out words, rather than the complicated codes in the French invention. This "Shutter Telegraph" as it was known, could be seen at a distance of ten miles on a clear day and an average message could be transmitted in this way from London to Portsmouth in fifteen minutes or less. Several lines of these Shutter Stations were built; one was at Blandford, the current site of the Royal School of Signals.

In 1796 a chain of telegraph stations, each of which used a frame containing six tilting wooden boards or shutters, was in operation between the Admiralty and Sheerness, Deal and Portsmouth. In October 1805 the decision was taken to extend the system from Beacon Hill at Portsmouth to Plymouth. There were many sites to select and prove workable in difficult country and winter weather, but by May 1806 the line was virtually ready. Eventually there were 64 shutter telegraph posts in England.

The full complement of a main shutter station was usually a Lieutenant Royal Navy (in charge), a Midshipman and two assistants (known as 'jack-tars' or 'foremastmen'). Not all Midshipmen were young.

The duties of the crew are partly explained in a lady's fan of the period. It shows the movements of the shutters above the hut and the persons within it. The officer is writing down the message in a ledger, the midshipman is standing at the telescope and one or both foremastmen are looking after the ropes. If only one 'jack-tar' was required to operate the ropes, the other would be charged with looking through his glass in the opposite direction.

The glass men did not have to have their eyes glued all the time, but they did have to keep watch every five minutes. The operators soon acquired great skill. A message between London and Portsmouth might take about fifteen minutes to pass. As with the later semaphore, the shutter spelled the words but often contracted them,

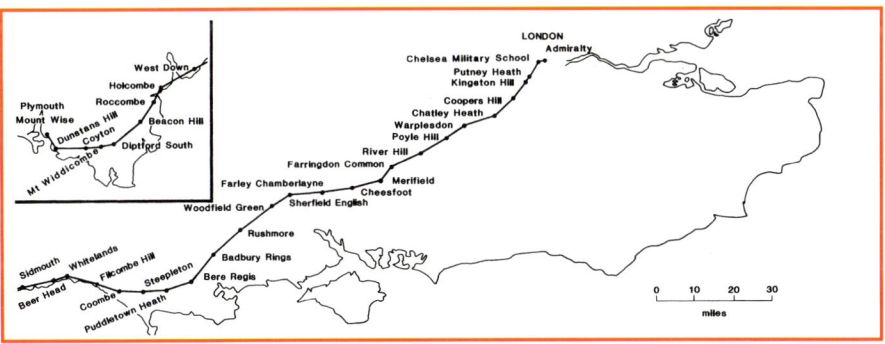

Several lines of Murray's Shutter Stations were built; each station used a frame containing six tilting wooden shutters. The map above shows the 22-station route from London to Plymouth proposed in 1822; eventually there were no less than 64 shutter telegraph posts in England

15

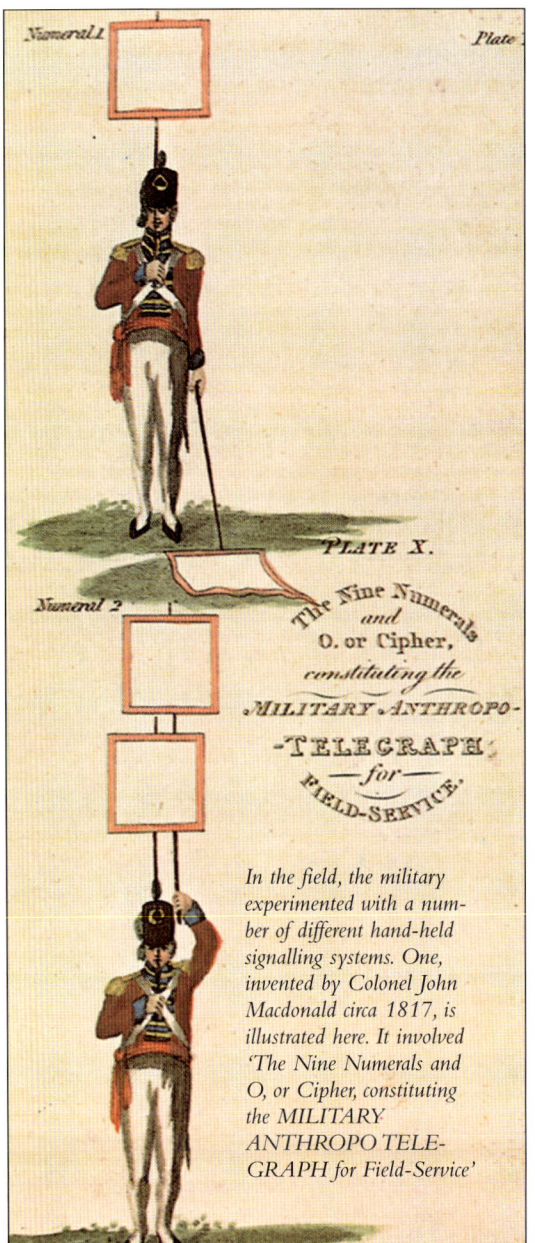

PLATE X.

The Nine Numerals and O. or Cipher, constituting the MILITARY ANTHROPO- -TELEGRAPH —for— FIELD-SERVICE.

In the field, the military experimented with a number of different hand-held signalling systems. One, invented by Colonel John Macdonald circa 1817, is illustrated here. It involved 'The Nine Numerals and O, or Cipher, constituting the MILITARY ANTHROPO TELE-GRAPH for Field-Service'

leaving out some of the vowels. A preparative signal could be sent from London to Deal or Portsmouth and acknowledged back in two minutes. A similar pre-arranged signal is said to have passed from London to Plymouth and back in three minutes.

Life could be difficult for the crews of the shutter stations, especially when it was windy or in very cold weather when the shutters tended to stick and would have to be manually freed. But on fine days, the life must have had many of the advantages and none of the drawbacks of life on board ship.

From 1806 to 1845 the day to day running of the tele-graph was the responsibility of John Barrow (later Sir John Barrow, Bt), Second Secretary at the Admiralty. Barrow also super-vised the correspondence with naval officers all over the world and with agents of other boards.

Paul Piggott and Frederick Locker

In 1840, visibility in London was much worse than it is today. The Admiralty Telegraph Station in London was often unable to send or receive messages for reasons officially given as "smoke", "state of atmos-

16

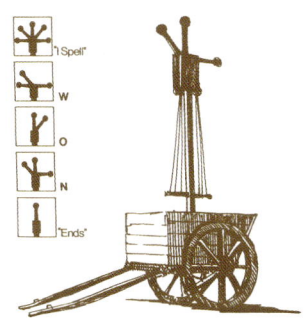

Outstanding among the first mobile communications systems was the Radiated Telegraph, above, invented by the Reverend John Gamble, the Chaplain General. Purchased by the Army in 1797, this was strictly a semaphore, defined as 'a signalling apparatus comprised of post with arms'

phere to the eastward", or "vapour arising from the lake in St James's Park". During the years 1838-1840, there were 133 days when the telegraph could not be used.

Simon Piggott's son Paul was fortunate in having received an elementary education and much encouragement from his parents. With the promise of an apprenticeship in London to a firm of shipping agents, he travelled to the capital and took lodgings with Frederick Locker, Deputy Reader at the Admiralty.

Paul knew about the telegraph from his father but now heard how, when the weather was bad, messages were carried from the Admiralty Station to Chelsea by messengers for onward transmission. If the weather was still bad at Chelsea, the messengers would continue to Putney where conditions were sometimes better. Messages arriving at Putney from Plymouth and Portsmouth in poor weather were carried over to

Chelsea by the gardener from a nearby house. For this he was paid 1s.

In summer the times of watch were from 10 to 5pm; during the winter the watch ended at 3pm. Frederick Locker started work at the Admiralty at 8.15am when he began to open the mail. He had until 10 o'clock to complete this task, for the Lords at the Admiralty could not send messages until after 10am.

In the mid 19th Century, the Navy was a shadow of the power it had been during the Napoleonic Wars. From 142,100 seamen and marines in 1810, the numbers had fallen by 1817 to a mere 22,944 and only 13 ships of the line. By the middle of the century, the average age of an Admiral had increased to 76 and the Navy List was clogged with ageing captains with nothing to do but draw their half pay.

The Gamble Radiated Telegraph was used both in the Peninsular campaign of 1811, as illustrated, and also as a means of communication from London to the East Coast. Some years after his death in 1811 an improved version was adopted by the Royal Navy. Remarkably, this was still being used during World War Two!

CHAPTER TWO

The credit for the Shutter Telegraph belongs to Claude Chappe. The semaphore (meaning 'bear a sign') was the invention of another Frenchman, Depillon, who evolved it in 1801 for ship to shore communication by means of two pivoting arms mounted directly on a mast. Admiral Sir Home Popham's arm-type telegraph was modelled on this.

The French never lost sight of the distinction between semaphore and telegraph because their coast semaphore system developed quite independently of the already established overland shutter telegraph system. But in England, the two systems were often confused, and the telegraph stations with their movable shutters were often referred to as "semaphore stations". In fact, both semaphore and shutter were telegraph systems, i.e. a means of communicating messages across distance according to some arranged code.

The dictionary defines semaphore as "Signalling apparatus comprised of post with arms used in military and railway signalling." A shutter telegraph system on the other hand was larger and more complex and consisted of several boards which could be 'opened' and 'closed' in many different combinations.

No sooner had the semaphore been thought of than it was imitated by many other inventors, most seeking to adapt its simple principle to telegraphy. Semaphores were devised with three or even four arms on a post. These arms might be displayed just on one side of the post in which case each would be capable of three changes. If arms were displayed on both sides of the post, the variations would be six in each case. With three separate arms using both sides, there were 301 combinations.

Admiral Sir Home Popham introduced his sea telegraph (an apparatus of semaphore type for mounting on ships and the predecessor of his similar land telegraph machine) in 1816. That was the year when Admiral Sir Edward Pellew sailed from Plymouth in his Flagship *Queen Charlotte* with five ships of the Line. His little known action against the Algerians resulted in the release of Christian slaves.

It was not until 1870 that the semaphore and sea telegraph devices became at all widespread and by that time, the original Popham design had been superseded by the more advanced Paisley design.

The heyday of seaborne semaphore was at the beginning of the 20th Century when the bridges of virtually all warships, British and others, bristled with such signalling machines while members of the crew communicated with handflags. But nobody really considered sea semaphore suitable for long distance communication although for a brief spell there was a huge masthead semaphore with 12ft arms meant for long distance work.

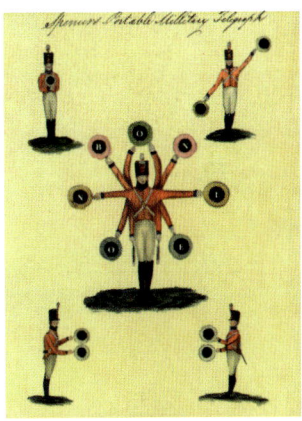

Mr Knight Spencer's invention from Ms. Transactions of the Society of Arts, 1808-09

The first mobile communications

Meanwhile The Chaplain General, the Reverend John Gamble, formerly a mathematics don at Pembroke College, Cambridge, invented a Radiated Telegraph which he sold to the Army in 1797. This machine was more mobile than the Murray Telegraph and was used both in the Peninsular campaign and also as a means of communication from London to the East Coast. Gamble hoped that the Navy would use his machine for ship to shore signalling but found the Admiralty unimpressed. However, some years after his death in 1811, Sir Charles Paisley, an Army General, succeeded in having an improved Gamble machine adopted by the Navy. Surprisingly, this machine was still in use in the 1940s.

The Anthropo Day and Night portable Telegraph

THE ELECTRIC TELEGRAPH

The electric telegraph was invented in the mid-19th Century, when the rapidly expanding international rail network needed to convey messages from point to point along the track. In 1819 the Danish H C Oersted found that if a current was passed through a conductor near a needle, the latter would deflect in different ways depending on the current flow direction. This enabled the Italian Galvani to produce a machine in which the 26 letters of the alphabet were pointed to by magnetic needles at the ends of 26 wires. William Sturgeon produced the first electro-magnet in 1825, and within six years had demonstrated an electro-magnetic signalling apparatus.

The first practical telegraph in the UK was installed between Euston and Camden Stations in 1837, a distance of one mile/1.6km, by two scientists, Cooke and Wheatstone. Within three years this system was being operated in the US by some 50 companies.

Wheatstone also introduced Britain's first automatic sending and receiving apparatus. This increased the human operator's sending speed tenfold, and provided more signalling capacity down a single line. One further refinement came shortly after 1851, when the professor of music who invented the microphone, Professor D E Hughes, also designed a type-writing telegraph. This pre-dated the typewriter, and was the forerunner of the teleprinter.

used discs and was the invention of Mr Knight Spencer, a Captain in the London Volunteers, who received the Royal Society's Silver Medal for it in 1809. It was the forerunner of the ordinary hand semaphore, on which the Army and Navy relied well into the 20th Century. Like those used in the Royal Navy, the signals were numerical and every kind of communication could be made up to a distance of three miles with virtually no possibility of error.

Every invention seems to produce a controversy and there was a long lasting argument between the supporters of the single letter type of signals and the code-sending signal. Both claimed that the other was the slower and less efficient method. However, in either form, this semaphore type of signalling was never much used in the Army. It was too slow, limited in range and made the signaller too easy a target. Nevertheless, it proved a lasting test of prowess in the Boy Scouts and as a signalling 'arm' had a long and successful history on the railways.

Electric signals

The possibility of using electricity to carry signals was identified by the mid-18th Century but sufficient electric charge could not be generated or stored to signal further than a few metres. The situation changed in 1800 with the invention of the electric battery, followed in 1819 by electro-magnets. In 1837, William Cooke and Charles Wheatstone produced the first practical electric telegraph system in Britain. An electric current travelling along a wire deflected a needle enabling a message to be transmitted. The system was used by the new railway companies who were able to send messages between signal boxes using telegraph lines beside the track.

It was at about the same time in the United States that the artist and inventor Samuel Morse perfected his own electric telegraph system; his most famous invention, however, was the code named after him which he had devised by 1838 but did not patent for another seventeen years. The Morse Code of dots and dashes provided for the first time a standard system for signalling which could transmit any message, be read by ear or eye and could be transmitted by any medium. The British Army adopted the Morse Code. Now they had a system which could convey messages quickly and accurately over long distances in any condition. The modern era of communications had dawned.

The Heliograph

The use of reflected sunlight to flash messages has a long history. During the wars between the Greeks and the Persians, polished shields were used, and Native Americans used pieces of silica and mica to flash signals.

In the 18th Century, the British Secret Service, one of whose members was Dr Benjamin Franklin, may have had a network of heliograph stations. He was a man of many parts, starting his working life as a printer and later becoming involved in politics and science. The lightning conductor was invented by him and it was he who first used the electrical terms 'positive', 'negative', 'battery' and 'conductor'.

"3rd June 1778. Did this day heliograph intelligence from Dr Franklin in Paris to Wycombe" ... so wrote John Hawley from Hawley Park in Camberley in Surrey.

It is not generally known that Franklin was a secret agent for the British Secret Service. The naval and military intelligence which he collected was relayed by devious routes to Lord Despencer at West Wycombe. As well as being members of the Hell-

---

MORSE CODE

Samuel Morse, 1791-1872, was a professor of painting and sculpture. In 1832, he experimented with the recording of electrical signals by fitting a pencil to a lever worked by an electro-magnet; the pencil struck and marked a continuously moving strip of paper. He called this the Morse Code, the code consisting of letters being represented by a combination of dots and dashes, representing short and long pulses of electrical current, light or sound. The most common letters had the smallest number of symbols. In 1843 the US Congress allocated $30,000 for the construction of an experimental line between Washington DC and Baltimore, Maryland. It was completed the following year, and in May Morse sent his first message – *What God hath wrought!* Morse was granted his first patent in 1848; within three years his system was being operated by 50 US companies. Later, he was involved in litigation over his claim to have invented the telegraph; the courts decided in his favour. He next experimented with submarine cable telegraphy, before dying in New York on 2 April 1872.

A . –	B – . . .	C – . – .	D – . .	E .	F . . – .	G – – .
H	I . .	J . – – –	K – . –	L . – . .	M – –	N – .
O – – –	P . – – .	Q – – . –	R . – .	S . . .	T –	U . . –
V . . . –	W . – –	X – . . –	Y – . – –	Z – – . .		

Fire Club, both men had something else in common; they had both been Postmasters General in their own countries.

So how did the messages pass from Paris and Camberley? Not far from Chichester Harbour stands Racton Monument, built in 1772. To the north on a ridge of the South Downs are the ruins of another. From there, the tower at Leigh Hill would have been easy to see with the top 1,000ft above sea level. If a heliograph had been operated, all these points could have been used and many more not mentioned here.

The prototype of the modern Heliograph was the Heliotrope which was invented by the German Karl Dauss in 1821. It was a surveying instrument which consisted of two mirrors at right angles which were used to transmit a steady beam of light to a distant station.

In the 1860s the British added a shutter to the Heliotrope which allowed the beam of light to be interrupted so Morse Code could be transmitted.

In 1869, Sir Henry Manse replaced the fixed mirror and shutter with an oscillating mirror; this was the first Heliograph. It was widely used in India and Africa in the late 19th Century.

Heliographs were frequently employed during World War One. The last recorded use by the British Army was at the Siege of Solom in North Africa in 1941.

The heliograph, where sunlight is reflected off a polished surface or mirror to send messages, has been in use throughout military history. In the 19th Century, the British Army adapted a German two-mirror surveying instrument by adding a shutter – replaced by an oscillating mirror in 1869 – which enabled it to transmit Morse Code. Here signallers are using 10" and 5" heliographs during the South African War

FROM THE CRIMEAN TO
THE BOER WAR

Cable wagons and cable carts were used to lay the 21 miles of cable wire which connected the eight telegraph offices on the circuit which linked Lord Raglan's Crimean headquarters with the War Office in London

Morse's electric telegraph was first used in war in the Crimea. In 1854, a 340 mile submarine cable joined Balaclava, where British and French were confronting the Russians, to Varna, where the British force had a base. From Varna there was an overland system which connected the Commanders in Chief with Paris and London. Forward telegraph communications were provided by 26 Regiment Royal Engineers (RE). They established a series of telegraph offices linked by insulated copper cable.

The telegraph link enabled the French Emperor Napoleon III to burden his commanders in chief with unnecessary suggestions and enquiries. Not to be outdone, the British War Office was adding to the already heavy burden of the Commander in Chief by requests for the sort of information which a modern commander might reasonably expect but which drove the unfortunate General Simpson to exasperation. He complained 'the confounded telegraph has ruined everything'.

Captain Robert Locker was the cousin of Frederick Locker, a Deputy Reader at the Admiralty, and was a member of the RE Telegraph Detachment sent to the Crimea in 1854 where his work included supervising the cable laying in the Crimea. Later in life, he often reflect-

23

ed back on those days and enjoyed telling his son William about his exploits.

"Our most difficult assignment?", mused Colonel Locker, "well, we were used to tackling most things, but I think that cable-laying operation in the Crimea was the most extraordinary business I've ever been involved in. It was 1854 and our Regiment's Telegraph Detachment had to lay both submarine and overland cables linking our troops at Balaclava first under the Black Sea to Lord Raglan in the British base at Varna, then overland all the way to England and 10 Downing Street".

Conditions in the Crimea were often terrible. It was either freezing cold or baking hot, and in either case, the ground was often so hard that the cable could not be laid in the conventional way with a plough. The men were issued with spades and had to dig the trench themselves.

"Rations were of the skimpiest; I was often reduced to bread and biscuit, with a raw onion to follow, although we could sometimes buy very good coffee. It's a wonder we had the strength to haul the cable drum onto the cart, let alone lay it!

And we had to keep on the alert all the time. There could be sudden attacks by the Russians, or raids by the thieving Turks who pinched the copper wire to use as clothes lines. Eventually, though, we managed to lay it, all 21 miles (33.5kms) of it, and set up eight telegraph offices. And didn't this just give the politicians their chance to interfere! The French officers told me that their Emperor was constantly bombarding his officers with orders and advice, while our damned War Office wasn't far behind.

But the real cream of the jest came when our Government sent their first message to Lord Raglan. The old boy made a real occasion of it, I was told, telling all his staff to assemble while he sent an official reply. All were assembled, and the message arrived. His Lordship took it with an air of great importance, to find it was in code – and he had lost the cipher! Staff officers and orderlies flew left and right, but to no avail. It had disappeared for ever. He was obliged to telegraph London, not

Cable ploughs were used to bury the cable in the Crimea to protect it from sabotage. It was during the Crimean War, 1854-5, that the electric telegraph was used for the first time

with a grand reply, but with a sheepish request for another copy of the code before he could read their message! Somehow it made all our hard work worth while".

The RE Telegraph Detachment which went into the Crimea in 1854 was equipped with two telegraph wagons and a cart which carried a drum of cable mounted in such a way as to make laying the cable easier. Originally it was intended to lay the cable into furrows made by a cable-plough. However the ground was too hard and the Sappers had to resort to digging with spades. As a result, they could not bury their telegraph cable very deep and the insulation was frequently eaten by mice or used by soldiers to repair their pipes. They also learned fairly quickly that the copper wire was also appreciated by local inhabitants who removed it as soon as the line-layers departed and used it for domestic purposes.

The single-needle telegraph instrument employed could be operated at approximately fifteen words per minute. In modern terminology this equates to 12 bits/s.

The Abyssinian War of 1867 brought further active service experience for the field telegraphists and signallers of the RE. The 10th Company RE was reinforced by field telegraphists and visual signallers from the RE base at Chatham, along with personnel from the Indian Sapper and Miner Telegraph Sections. They provided communications by means of Morse, flag and lamp signalling.

The formation of a Signal Service owed much to the lobbying of Field Marshal Sir John Fox Burgoyne. He was Lord Raglan's Chief Engineer in the Crimea and later was Inspector General of Fortifications. He believed in the importance of good communication in the field. His recommendation that a Signal Service be formed was based on evidence from the American Civil War.

Permission was given in 1869 for the formation of a Signal Wing at the RE's depot at Chatham. Six years later, the Wing was split and the Instructor-in-Army-Signalling moved to Aldershot to form a school of visual signalling. From 1886 onwards, this school formed part of the infantry organisation.

The Instructor-in-Telegraph continued to be based in Chatham and was responsible for electrical signalling. This split in responsibilities lasted until 1909 when, after the Boer War, all signalling became a Royal Engineer responsibility. In 1870, the War Office decided that a unit was needed to provide telegraph communications for the Field Army. 'C' Troop RE was formed with a complement of five officers, 245 other ranks and 115 horses, with four office wagons for the telegraph equipment and eight general purpose wagons for stores. Field Marshal Kitchener of Khartoum served in Blandford as a Lieutenant in this unit from April 1873 until October 1874.

At the same time as 'C' Telegraph Troop was formed, the Government also decided that it would buy the private telegraph companies in the United Kingdom

THE TELEPHONE

During the mid-19th Century many inventors claimed to have created "electrical speech", and in 1861 the German Philip Reis came close to perfecting the first telephone instrument. Among the items used were a knitting needle, an animal membrane, sealing wax, platinum and a violin! But although Reis managed to convey sound at a constant pitch, he could not convey speech. This was first achieved by a Scottish emigrant, Alexander Graham Bell – 1847-1922 – whose family had settled in Massachusetts. He conducted his experiments in a noisy electrical workshop, siting himself in the attic and his assistant in the basement. In 1875 Bell had experimented with ideas for a dot-and-dash telegraph working over a single wire – earth return telegraphy – and while testing one of his devices he heard a twanging sound accidentally caused by his assistant at the other end. He realised that not only could dots and dashes be transmitted over wires, but speech also. The following year he built his first practical telephone instrument. This was on the same principle as a modern telephone, with a microphone comprising a horn-like speaking tube, at the narrow end of which was a diaphragm that moved a coil within an electro-magnet and induced a variable direct current – dc – voltage, produced from a battery, into a telephone line. At the other end was a receiver with a diaphragm driven by the speech currents which turned the electrical signal back into sound waves audible to the listener. The first spoken words are reputed to have been *"Mr Watson, come here, I want you"*. From that day on, experiments were conducted on both sides of the Atlantic. Among those involved were Thomas Edison – 1847-1931 – and the English Professor D E Hughes, who greatly improved speech quality by inventing what he christened the carbon microphone.

Bell demonstrated his telephone at the 1876 Centennial Exposition in Philadelphia, and formed his own firm, the Bell Telephone Company, in 1877. His other inventions included the photophone for transmitting speech by light rays, the audiometer for measuring human hearing, and in 1886 the first wax recording cylinder – the basis of the gramophone.

because they had proved to be inefficient in private hands. So it was that in 1870 all these companies were integrated into the General Post Office Telegraph Company. In 1879 the National Telephone Company was born; it was incorporated into the General Post Office (GPO) on 1 January 1912. However, at the outset it was desperately short of skilled personnel and it was suggested that the RE could help get the organisation established and gain useful experience at the same time. The suggestion was accepted and the 22nd Company RE was loaned to the GPO. Later the 34th Company RE was also made available to serve with the Postal Telegraphs. It was the beginning of a close relationship between the Armed Services and the GPO and more recently British Telecommunications plc (BT) which has lasted until the present day.

In 1872, 'C' Telegraph Troop was involved in an Army exercise set in Southern England. The Troop set up its Headquarters in the Blandford area. Meanwhile, the Postal Telegraph Companies gained their first war service experience in 1873 when a detachment took part in the expedition led by Sir Garnet Wolseley into Ashanti to deal with King Coffee Kalkali, a noted slave trader.

'C' Telegraph Troop

When 'C' Troop RE was formed in 1870 it was equipped with twelve wire wagons, each drawn by six horses. By 1890 these wagons were called cable wagons and smaller, faster Cable Carts, drawn by two horses, were in service. In 1911 the Cable Cart was taken out of service and all Signals Units were supplied with an improved version of the cable wagon.

Early Telephones

It was at the Centennial Exhibition at Philadelphia in the autumn of 1876 that the telephone invented by Alexander Graham Bell was first publicly unveiled. The scientist Sir William Thompson hailed it as the greatest marvel yet achieved by the electric telegraph. Others were more disparaging and complained that to be heard at all 'one had to shout oneself hoarse'. This was not surprising because the microphone had not then been invented.

The new invention excited the interest of the officers of the RE and in 1877 Mr Preece, founder of the London-Paris telephone line, brought back some instruments from America and showed them to the Telegraph Troop Officers in the RE Theatre at Aldershot.

Lieutenant A W Bagnold, RE, immediately constructed a home made telephone which he described in the RE Journal of November 1877 (See Appendix Two).

Meanwhile, 'do it yourself' production was in full swing in India. Major General J E Dickie, CB, CMG wrote that when he joined the Bengal Sappers and Miners at Roorkee in 1877 there was a school of Signalling there under Lieutenant G R R Savage RE. In the workshops there were skilled Indian artisans who, under the supervision of Lieutenant Savage and Sergeant Miller, made the signalling equipment, mainly heliographs and new telephones on the Bell pattern.

Each of the offices in the telegraph sections of the companies was equipped with two telephones, ten miles of copper wire carried on jointed bamboo poles and a quan-

QUEEN VICTORIA'S FIRST TELEPHONE

An extract from *The Times* of 16 January, 1878, describes how the telephone was first demonstrated to Queen Victoria.

The Telephone at Court. On Monday evening (January 14) as announced in the Court Circular, Professor Bell and Colonel Reynolds were presented to the Queen, and exhibited the telephone, being assisted by Mr C Wollaston. In a lecture of 15 minutes duration Professor Bell explained the mechanism of his invention and then held telephonic communication with Osborne-cottage, the residence of Sir Thomas Biddulph.

Her Majesty conversed with Sir Thomas and Lady Biddulph and later Miss Kate Field, who was at Osborne-cottage, sang "Kathleen Mavourneen" for which Her Majesty returned gracious thanks telephonically through the Duke of Connaught. Miss Field afterwards sang Shakespeare's "Cuckoo Song" and "Coming through the Rye" and delivered the epilogue to "As you Like It" all of which were heard distinctly. The applause which followed came through the telephone.

The Princess Beatrice, the Hon Mrs Ponsonby, and others conversed with Osborne-Cottage, sometimes through a circuit of one, three and five persons. As the evening wore on, telephonic connexion was established between Osborne-house and Cowes, Southampton and London. At Cowes, where Major Webber of the RE superintended the line, a quartet of tonic-sol-fa singers, consisting of Miss Webber, Miss Strohmeinger, Mr Hamilton and Mr Curwen, sang several part songs which produced an admirable effect and the Duke of Connaught talked for several minutes with Major Webber. Attention was then turned to Southampton, where Mr W H Preece of the Post Office talked as fluently with Professor Bell and Colonel Reynolds as though he were in the next room. A bugle in Southampton sounded the retreat with startling distinctness and, lastly, came the tones of the organ from London in charge of Mr Wilmot. The experiments lasted from half past nine until nearly midnight. Her Majesty, the Princess Beatrice, the Duke of Connaught and the entire Royal household evinced the greatest interest.

tity of insulated cable.

In 1877, the results of the Dehra Dun races were telephoned successfully to Roorkee, the telegraph lines having been borrowed for the occasion!

The Bengal Sappers and Miners were not slow to take the telephone into the field. In December 1877 a field telegraph detachment built a telegraph route from Peshawar to Matanni and then to the main camp below Sargasha – over 30 miles in length. This was the first recorded use of telephones in war in the British and Indian Armies. Bearing in mind reports in Britain that same year that a new design telephone would work at distances of about a mile, Lieutenant Savage's home made telephone was an exceptionally good one.

Later, telephones were installed in Royal Garrison Artillery Fortresses in Britain. It took some time for British officers to accept the new instrument because the early telephones were unreliable and there was no written copy of the messages sent.

The Zulu Wars

'C' Telegraph Troop first saw active service in the Zulu War of 1879 when, under the command of Major A C Hamilton, seven officers, 200 men and 110 horses moved from the United Kingdom to Africa to provide communications for the campaign. The Troop used hand-speed morse-sounders and morse-recorders as well as the high-speed Wheatstone Automatic System. They kept the headquarters of an advancing force in contact with base by laying insulated telegraph cable along the line of advance, initially on the ground; overhead cable came later. During their service in Zululand, the troops were also issued with four heliographs which had been made by the Bengal Sappers and Miners in their workshop at Roorkee, India.

The telephone also played a part in the campaign as extracts from the Historical Records of 'C' Telegraph Troop reveal:

12 July 1879

A line commenced to Conference Hill thirteen miles on from Kopjie Allein with copper wires on bamboos, and completed the following day. Owing to defective insulation and want of battery power, it was found necessary to put telephones on the line with ordinary sounders. This worked well.

14 July 1879

A line was commenced towards Stelezi and six miles poled the remaining four

This 1992 painting by Peter Archer shows Royal Engineer signallers at the Tugela River in 1879, establishing contact with the beleaguered British force in Fort Ekowe by heliograph

miles was placed on the ground and the line was worked with telephone.

In a letter dated 25 November 1880, Major A C Hamilton, Officer Commanding 'C' Troop, reported that he had experimented several times with the telephone produced in 1878 by the Telephone Company (this was the one with a projected distance of one mile) but said that the only time it had any useful result was on the line between Kopjie Allein and Conference Hill. 'In the early morning when the dew was on the ground the current went to earth but by putting the telephone on the ground, the working of the Morse instruments could be distinctly heard and messages read off in that way'. This technique is known as "earth return" telegraphy and it is still used today.

During the campaign, part of the British force became beleaguered at Fort Ekowe, with the ground between the Fort and the Tugela River being held by the Zulu army. At Tugela, Lieutenant Haynes RE spent a week heliographing in the direction of the Fort. Eventually he received an answer from the Fort due to the perseverance of Major E T Wynne RE who had noticed the signal almost immediately. First, he tried to return a signal by the use of shaving mirrors, but when this did not work, he spent a week constructing a large screen which pivoted from the horizontal to the vertical, thus producing the elements of Morse Code. As a result, the Fort was relieved.

The Second Afghan War

The Defence of Sherpur was the first time that the telephone was used in siege operations. At that time the word 'telegraph' was being used to cover communications by sounder or telephone. In the summer of 1879 General Dickie became Superintendent of Field Telegraphy to Sir Donald Stewart's Kandahar Field Force .

Dickie described how this Force made contact with the other British/Indian Force by flashing two helio mirrors in the direction which the topography suggested would be the direction it was coming from. They established contact within five minutes. The report and casualty lists were immediately passed and appeared in the *Times* the following day. The Kandahar Field Force were in touch with Kabul by heliograph from a commanding hill. The signal traffic was telephoned from Force Headquarters in the valley up to the helio station.

The Egyptian Campaign

By 1882 the telephone had become part of the standard equipment in the Telegraph Battalion, R.E. News of the victory at Tel-el-Kebir was telegraphed to the Queen by Sir Garnet Wolseley over a system using the Theiber sounder and telephone. His message was timed 0700 hrs but was handed in at the wrong office and not transmitted until 08.30 hrs. The Queen's reply was received at 09.15 hrs. Notwithstanding the initial delay, it was a good performance! It was the first victory signal ever to come direct from a battlefield.

In 1884 'C' Troop and the Postal Telegraph Companies were formally amalgamated to become 1 and 2 Division The Telegraph Battalion. They were formed from units which had served with distinction in the Colonial Wars of the late 19th Century, including the two RE companies that had been formed in 1870 and 1871 to help construct and operate the GPO's Public Telegraph Service. Major C F C Beresford RE who commanded the newly formed 2nd Division asked for suggestions for a device or crest for the Telegraph Battalion. His own suggestion of the figure of Mercury proved to be the most popular and was adopted for use on special occasions and on

Mr H R Forster's letter to the Editor of The Times c1880, recommending the use of the telephone for military communication in the field as more efficient than the 'mirror telegraph'

notepaper headings. It still appears as the badge of the Royal Corps of Signals.

In his report on the expedition to the Eastern Sudan in 1885, Major Beresford recommended that 'a number of telephones should always be taken into the field. They are useful for a short branch line to departments and save trained telegraphists as anyone can communicate by them'.

Telephones were still not particularly popular with commanders and

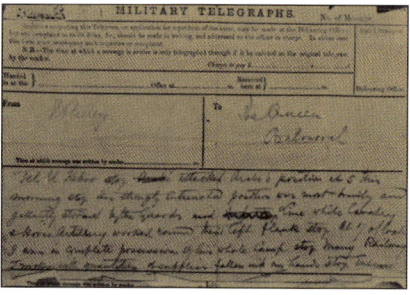

This telegram from Sir Garnet Wolseley to Queen Victoria at Balmoral reported victory at Tel-el-Kebir in 1882, and was the first to be sent direct from a battlefield

staff whether in peacetime or at war. They still preferred to have written proof in the form of a telegraph message and complained that it was difficult to write down a telephoned message while holding the telephone. It took Beresford some time to overcome this resistance.

The Telegraph Battalion supplied sections for the Bechuanaland[1], Nile and Suakin[2] expeditions and at the Battle of Tofrek[3], electric telegraph was used for the

The interior of a signallers' telegraph tent during fighting in the Sudan, 1896-98.

[*] See footnotes at end of chapter.

first time in the front line. The Royal Engineer Signallers became skilled in building long telegraph lines and improving existing civilian systems. They were aided by the new Airline system which consisted of a single wire conductor carried on lightweight poles which could be built at the rate of six to eight miles a day (See 'Earth Return Telegraphy' on page 45, Chapter Four).

The signallers became highly skilled operators and in one night during the Nile Expedition, one telegraph office handled 550 messages.

During the fourth Ashanti War of 1895/6, Major R S Curtis RE took 52 men to provide the communications for the force which was sent to remove King Prempeh 1 from the throne of Ashanti. The King was generally believed to be indulging in human sacrifice and cannibalism.

The men from the Telegraph Battalion hacked a path for the cable line through the jungle. Two out of every three men were stricken with fever and the remainder struggled on to Kumassi, the capital, 145 miles from their base at Cape Coast.

Finally when King Prempeh was seated in his sacrificial grove awaiting the coming of the 'red coats', Sergeant J L Low with two other men in blue carrying a drum of cable came out of the jungle and erected their blue and white signal office flag in the centre of the grove. They had arrived in advance of the main force and signalled back to Major Curtis that they had reached the capital. As a reward, General Sir Francis Scott gave the King's chair to the small detachment; later this was given to the Royal Signals by Major General Sir Reginald Curtis.

The Boer War

The Telegraph Battalion was responsible throughout the Campaign for keeping their headquarters connected to the civil network as well as for repairing and extending the lines.

Reinforcements for the Battalion were provided by complete sections drafted from Britain. This simplified their rapid deployment on active service.

The Wheatstone Automatic Telegraph was used for heavy traffic. It is recorded that one instrument cleared 6,000 words in 105 minutes, (equal in

Tony Theobald's painting shows the Wheatstone Automatic Morse Telegraph equipment in use during the Boer War, 1899-1902

THE TELEPHONE RELAY*

*Relay = Message received from and originating at another exchange

Hans Christian Oersted - 1777-1851 - Professor of Physics at the University of Copenhagen, discovered in 1819 that a magnetic needle is deflected at right angles to a wire carrying an electric current. This was taken a stage further by Michael Faraday - 1791-1867 - who in 1821 plotted the magnetic field around a conductor carrying an electric current. Between them, they established the basic principles of the electro-magnet, i.e. when a wire coil carrying a direct current - dc - is wound around a core of soft iron, a magnetic field is created which mirrors that of a permanent magnet. When the current is switched off, the magnetic field collapses and disappears. The soft iron core can be made to attract a similar armature, which has many uses, such as the electrical relay, or mechanical switch operated by a direct current.

The first electro-magnet was produced by William Sturgeon, a Lancashire shoemaker and keen experimenter, in 1825. Within six years, electro-magnetic signalling apparatus had been manufactured. A variety of relays for telegraphic use were produced after 1837 by the Ericsson Company of Sweden, while in the UK the Automatic Telephone Company introduced the Strowger Automatic Telephone Relay after the design of the Strowger two-motion telephone selector in 1891.

This had the layout of a modern telephone relay: soft iron core and yoke, large coil with several tens of thousands of windings, spring sets - contacts - for circuit switching, adjustable armature and residual. Later versions were introduced into the UK by Standard Telephones & Cables Ltd and the Siemens Company; and employed by the GPO mainly for manual switching. In 1932 the GPO introduced the standard Post Office relay, called the 3000 Type. This was widely used in automatic telephone equipment until electro-mechanical switching was abandoned in the UK during the late 1980s. (See also Automatic Telephone Switching)

---

modern terminology to 4800 bits/D or 4.8 kbit(s)) when the casualty list was sent after the battle of Magersfontein.

During the Boer War, the Telegraph Battalion section laid 18,000 miles of telegraph and telephone cable. A total of 13.5mn messages were handled in four years and the Battalion grew in strength from 600 to 2,500 men.

Extensive use of telephones in the latter stages of the campaign proved their military worth. Much use was made of the existing civilian telephones and telephone exchanges but for field use specially designed telephones and exchanges were produced. The C Mark 1 and the D Mark 1 were the first of a whole family of field telephones to be developed for the British Army.

General French used both telegraph and the telephone to direct his flank formations during the action at Bloemfontein and they were also used on the battlefield to control artillery fire. He attributed his victory to good communications. It was the first time that the Telegraph Battalion had provided tactical as well as strategic communications for the Army. It was also the first occasion in war when telephones were used in any number.

After Bloemfontein, the main war petered out. Lord Roberts divided his force into five columns marching on a front of 500 miles. Eight telegraph sections, using the Wheatstone, maintained communications between the columns. Three wagons were kept under the control of the headquarters and it was from this organisation that the idea of a Signal Corps later developed. From 1900 to 1902, the 'Guerrilla War' as it was then called, dragged on. During this last phase the country was divided by a chain of Block Houses linked by telephones operated by the Telegraph Battalion.

Some 9,360 miles of line were erected by men of the Telegraph Battalion and nearly 2,000 telephones were in use.

The South African War proved to be a milestone in the history of communications. Telegraphs were now recognised as an essential part of the modern army.

Wireless joins the forces

Throughout the 19th Century, men like Faraday, Maxwell and Hertz had carried out research into the properties of electro-magnetic waves. Their experiments had been carried out solely for the sake of scientific advance. It was Sir William Crookes – 1832-1919 – who first had the idea of using these waves for communication. Also experimenting at that time was Captain H B Jackson, a naval torpedo and electrical specialist. In 1895 he was appointed to command HMS *Defiance*, the torpedo school at Plymouth. By the end of the year he had constructed a wireless set, and was sending messages along a ship's length.

During 1896 he sent messages between two ships moored in harbour. In September he was present at Marconi's demonstration of his radio equipment on Salisbury Plain. The Italian government had not been interested in Marconi's work, so he had moved to England. Partly, this was because he could see that the greatest need for wireless was at sea. On land, the wireless and the telegraph appeared much the same

WIRELESS TELEGRAPHY

Many scientists experimented with newly discovered electricity and magnetism throughout the 19th Century. In 1864, the British Professor of Experimental Physics at Cambridge, James Clerk Maxwell – 1831-1879 – worked out mathematically that electro-magnetic waves obeyed the laws of natural light and travelled at the same speed of 186,000 miles per second. This was a great achievement, as he had no apparatus able to prove the theory! Twenty-four years later, the German Heinrich Hertz, 1857-1894, experimented with two rods with knobs on their ends, separated by an air gap, across which a high tension electrical current – spark – could jump. The waves created were very short, about 12"/300mm long, and although they could only propagate the length of his laboratory, wireless communication was born!

Towards the end of the century the young Italian electrician Guglielmo Marconi devised a method of transmitting and receiving electro-magnetic signals. He took his discovery to Britain in 1896, and received help from the Chief Engineer of the GPO, Sir William Preece, who had also been studying the phenomena. Soon after his arrival, Marconi demonstrated his invention by linking the GPO at St Martin's-le-Grand in London – the present site of BT Centre – with Queen Victoria Street, a distance of some 400 yards.

Marconi next produced signals across eight miles/12.9km of Salisbury Plain, and over nine miles/14.5km across the Bristol Channel. A year later, he succeeded in transmitting and receiving signals from ships at sea over 60 miles/96.5km away during naval manoeuvres. Wireless telegraphy stations were established in 1898 at Alum Bay on the Isle of Wight and at Bournemouth,

One of the great pioneers of communication, Guglielmo Marconi, 1874-1937

enabling Queen Victoria to keep in touch with her son Edward Prince of Wales on board the Royal Yacht *Osborne*. In March 1899 the English Channel was bridged by wireless, and in the same year wireless telegraphy was adopted by the Royal Navy and the Merchant Navy. In 1901 Marconi went even further. Using an aerial suspended from a kite, he transmitted a series of letter S's in Morse Code across the Atlantic from Poldhu in Cornwall to St Johns Newfoundland, a distance of nearly 2,000 miles/3,220km. Between 1907 and the end of WWI, wireless telegraphy – W/T – spread worldwide; in 1919 a message was successfully sent from England to Australia. The war had proved the worth of W/T, and stimulated future developments in wireless telephony and radio broadcasting.

MANUAL TELEPHONE SWITCHING

The first telephones communicated between only two fixed locations in a single area, and were directly connected by point-to-point lines: the equivalent of today's private wires or private circuits. It was soon realised that the efficiency of the service could be greatly improved and expanded by enabling any telephone to be connected to any other telephone in the neighbourhood. It was plainly impractical to run wires between every single telephone, and the obvious answer was to provide a central switching point. This was called an Exchange; each one was provided with a manual switchboard controlled by a large number of usually female telephonists, later called operators. The lines of subscribers connected to the service appeared on a jack-socket that was paralleled - multiplied - along a number of switchboards, and each had a calling indicator. Calls were connected by plugs and cords, and controlled by relays. Lifting the handset activated the calling indicator and attracted the operator's attention. Similarly, operators calling subscribers extended ringing current by means of a hand-cranked alternating current - ac - generator. The first small telephone exchange was opened in the City of London in 1879, while the GPO opened their first exchange in Swansea in 1881, closely followed by others in Newcastle-upon-Tyne, Bradford and Middlesbrough. Others were set up by private companies and some municipal authorities; the main ones were merged in 1889 to form the National Telephone Company. The GPO were given responsibility for all UK trunk calls in 1896; six years later they opened the first of several 14,000-line exchanges in central London. Finally the GPO absorbed the National Telephone Company in 1912, the same year they opened their first automatic exchange in Epsom, Surrey. By 1918 they operated over 819,000 telephones, virtually all manually switched.

thing. But at sea, once a ship was out of sight of land, it was completely isolated. With no cable link, there was no possibility of distress calls, hearing weather reports, relaying orders, or reporting sightings and actions. As it happened, electro-magnetic waves travelled better over the sea than over the land.

Captain Jackson benefited from his discussions with Marconi, and soon achieved a distance of three miles between the *Defiance* and Admiralty House, Plymouth. In March 1897 the Admiralty made a grant to the torpedo school to enable them to make wireless sets for trials with the fleet at sea. The Italian Navy also became interested at around the same time, but were slow to follow through and only purchased four sets from Marconi.

In 1899 Marconi sent messages across the Channel, a distance of 30 miles, and the French Navy became interested. The British torpedo school had no equipment ready for manoeuvres that year, so the Admiralty obtained three sets from Marconi, who attended the exercises. It soon became apparent that the easy exchange of wireless messages outdated the cumbersome older methods of visual signalling, shore signal stations and the telegraph. It also became obvious that electro-magnetic waves were not only projected into space, but followed the curvature of the earth, making even longer ranges possible. More than one radio channel could be used, and sets could be tuned to a secret frequency, preventing the enemy from listening in or jamming the transmissions.

Wireless was a great success, but the Admiralty found Marconi's financial conditions, especially the payment of royalties, unsatisfactory, so the Navy continued with their own experiments.

When the South African War broke out, the War Office obtained five sets from Marconi for use by the Army in the field. They were carried in horse-drawn wagons of the telegraph section of the RE, but were operated by Marconi personnel. They proved a failure; the aerials were unsatisfactory, atmospherics were poor and the hills interfered with communication. Enthusiasm within military circles waned although the Navy, who took over the same sets in February 1900, had some success with them.

One of the Navy's tasks was to blockade Portuguese Mozambique and German South-West Africa, preventing any supplies reaching the Boers; here wireless proved invaluable. One of the Marconi engineers reported that the officers found it useful for arranging future private engagcments! Wireless was even more useful on operations. A cruiser was stationed off Lourenco Marques, Mozambique's capital, while other warships patrolled, searching merchant vessels for contraband. Wireless kept all the ships in contact with each other, and with Simonstown naval base.

Wireless also helped prevent a conflict; when in May 1900 a cavalry regiment was preparing to land at Kosi Bay, the Consul-General at Lourenco Marques was able to send word that the Boers had learned of the plan.

By midsummer 1900, the Marconi sets had proved so superior to the Navy's own efforts that the Admiralty agreed to Marconi's terms and purchased 32, including the three used in South Africa. Most were installed in the Channel Squadron; six in the Mediterranean, four in the Reserve fleet and six for south coast shore stations in England and Ireland. By the end of the year, eight shore stations and 42 warships were equipped with wireless.

Meanwhile Captain Jackson was continuing to work on the 'service' sets. By January 1901 results were so improved that the Admiralty decided to use these as well as the Marconi equipment. In that year's naval manoeuvres, most of the ships taking part were fitted with wireless. Then in December came Marconi's remarkable achievement in sending a message across the Atlantic. Transmitted from Poldhu in Cornwall, the signals were picked up by a portable receiver in Newfoundland. He also produced a higher power transmitter, and a magnetic detector or 'Maggie', which could be used with headphones. This was much more sensitive as a receiver than the coherer, and allowed the speed of communication to be increased from ten to 20 words a minute.

The Navy were very keen to use Marconi's new transmitters, and in July 1903 signed an agreement to use his patent rights for a period of eleven years on payment of an annual sum, and to use the Poldhu station for 20 minutes every day. During 1904 the Navy converted or replaced all their existing sets in favour of the new transmitters. The same year, a wireless experimental section was formed at HMS *Vernon*, the torpedo school at Portsmouth, under Mr H B Madge, a former Marconi employee, with the objective of developing wireless equipment for the fleet. It was felt that Naval requirements were now so different from commercial ones that they needed specialised designs. By the end of the year they had produced a naval wireless set using an alternator in the transmitter and the 'Maggie' and telephones for reception. Wireless was no longer experimental; it had become established as a reliable international naval communication system.

In 1907, two wireless companies were formed and in 1908 the Evelyn Wood report was accepted. Rather than form a new corps, it was decided that the service would be best provided by a Royal Engineer Signal Service and this was formalised in 1910 when the existing 'Telegraph' Units were renamed 'Signal' Units.

By the outbreak of World War One the army had a small number of functioning wireless sets. They were mainly spark transmitters which operated on long waves and were cumbersome, heavy and unreliable.

The development of the thermionic valve enabled sets to be made which operated on medium and short waves. These transmitters and receivers were more reliable but still cumbersome. The Trench Spark Set – 50 watts (known as the B.F. Set) needed three men to carry the basic equipment and another three to handle the aerial gear and spare batteries.

By 1914, the Royal Flying Corps had begun to use wireless to direct artillery fire. An observer in the aircraft saw where the shots from the guns had fallen and signalled to the Artillery Controller on the ground using the Sparks Set. The Controller could then make the necessary adjustments to enable the guns to hit their target. Wireless was also used for Air Defence during the later years of the war for ground-to-air telephony. This was to be the major role of the Royal Flying Corps throughout the war.

Formation of the RE Signal Service

During the Boer War the independent and uncoordinated systems of communication led to rivalry and duplication of effort.

In 1905 the Telegraph Battalion was disbanded. Independent companies were formed from the men of the Battalion. In 1906, the Evelyn Wood Committee report recommended that the telegraph companies and the Army Signal Service should be combined to provide all forms of communications from battalion level back to base. The Reserve Army had been involved in telegraph communications for some years. Notably, there was the Post Office Volunteers which, as the 'General Post Office Rifles' provided a telegraph detachment for Sir Garnet Wolseley's force in the Egyptian campaign of 1882. This campaign won for the unit the first Volunteer overseas Battle Honour 'Egypt 1882'.

In 1912 Brigade Signal Sections were formed, responsible for communications from unit up to Brigade level. The Special Reserve produced the first motor cycle despatch riders. Corporals of the Reserve volunteered for this duty and provided their own machines. The Cambridge University Signal Section volunteered en masse as despatch riders in 1914.

Field Telephone Exchanges

The first telephones in military use were connected singly or in simple circuits of up to six instruments. This obviously limited their effectiveness. A number of telephones could be connected to an Exchange which allowed different telephone circuits to be inter-connected via a switchboard. Although switchboards were already in use to connect telegraph users, the military authorities were slow to adopt telephone exchanges and it was not until 1896 that the military installed the first military telephone switchboard. Within four years, 79 military switchboards were in use in the Boer War.

FOOTNOTES:

1 Now Botswana.

2 Suakin, ancient city on the Red Sea 50 miles south of Port Sudan.

3 Took place 22 March 1885 during the British Sudan campaign. Five thousand Mahdists attacked 2,000 British and Indian troops. In a fierce 20 minute fight, they lost 1,500 soldiers.

WORLD WAR ONE

Gilbert Holiday, one of the most accomplished action painters of horses, visited the Western Front as an unofficial War Artist in 1914 and later painted this picture of laying cable under fire in Flanders from sketches made on the spot

This war revolutionised communications. When war broke out in 1914 there were fewer than 6,000 men in the RE Signal Service. By the end of the war there were 70,000.

The war also saw the faltering beginnings of Britain's Air Defence System, the start of ground-to-air telephony and the increasingly important contribution made by the GPO in establishing telephone links between local operation centres and individual airfields. This was the first European war to be fought with the air dimension. By 1918, the Royal Air Force (RAF) had been established as the third arm of Britain's armed forces and warfare would never be the same again.

When the British Expeditionary Force (BEF) deployed at Mons on 22 August 1914, it included a GHQ Signal Company, two army corps headquarters signal companies, six divisional signal companies, one cavalry signal company, eight cable and five cable line sections and a lines of communication signal company. The total commitment was 75 officers and 2,346 men.

In 1914 the Signals Service was primarily a Telegraphic Service. But only four years later, the telephone was the main means of communication on the Western Front and wireless was playing a major part in military signalling.

The Signal Service was designed to operate with a moving army. During the mobile phase of the war, the cable detachments kept divisions and brigades in touch with each other by laying telegraph lines from their cable wagons, often under fire. But the growth of trench warfare entirely altered the requirement and the work grew out of all proportion. In 1914 a signal office at a corps headquarters would consider 100 messages a day as exceptional. By 1918, the average daily number was 4,500.

Telephones in World War One

At the beginning of the war, civilian telephones were pressed into front line service to meet the rapidly increasing need for communications. However they had not been designed to operate in damp, muddy conditions and as soon as possible, specially designed field magneto telephones for voice transmission, and buzzer telephones for Morse began to arrive on the Western Front.

The telephone D Mark 3 became the standard army telephone. It incorporated

The telephone switchboard on the castle ramparts at Montreuil, just inland from Boulogne, during World War One

a buzzer unit and a Morse key and so could be used to send and receive Morse if the circuit was too noisy for voice transmissions. Telephones could be easily overheard and thousands of casualties resulted from the interception of telephone conversations by the enemy until officers learned to use code when passing sensitive information. The cable was improved to prevent the leakage of signals and Captain (later Major General) A C 'Boney' Fuller invented the 'Fullerphone' in 1915 which made buzzer signals secure. They were still being used in the early stages of World War Two.

THE FULLERPHONE

Also known as the "Power Buzzer" this telegraphic instrument was used in war sig-nalling from the end of World War One to the early stages of World War Two. The essential point of the Fullerphone was the change at the receiving end of a steady current into an intermittent current of audible frequency, while at the same time the current in the line remained steady.

The telephone had proved itself in the latter stages of the Boer War and now came into its own in the trench system. Field telephones linked through manual exchanges became the principal means of communication in the Front Line either by speech or in Morse using the more secure buzzer phones. Wireless was also used but it was unpopular because the aerials attracted enemy fire and the early trench wireless sets were far from reliable.

Drawing of a typical trench dugout in 1915; the telegraphist can be seen handing his company command-er a message just received

Wireless

By the outbreak of war, the army had a small number of functioning wireless sets. They were mainly spark transmitters which operated on long wave and were cumbersome, heavy and unreliable.

The development of the thermionic valve enabled sets to be made which operated on medium and short waves. These transmitters were more reliable but still cumbersome. The Trench Spark Set – 50 watts (known as the B.F. Set) needed three men to carry the basic equipment and another three to handle the aerial gear and spare batteries.

The Royal Flying Corps (RFC) had been formed in May 1912 by amalgamating the air wings of the Royal Navy and the Army. By 1914 they had begun to use wireless to direct artillery fire. An observer in the aircraft plotted where the shots from the guns had fallen and signalled to the Artillery Controller on the ground using the Sparks Set. The Controller could then make the necessary adjustments to enable the guns to hit their target. Wireless was also used for Air Defence during the later years of the war for ground-to-air telephony. This was the major role of the Royal Flying Corps

THE THERMIONIC VALVE

While studying the reception of wireless radio signals, scientist John Flemming – 1849-1945 – examined the Edison Effect: how dark particles tended to smudge the inside of light bulbs when current flowed through them in one direction. He decided to fit a bulb with a second set of electrodes – filaments – and link it to a radio receiver. In the rectifying vacuum tube he produced in 1900, Flemming observed that electrons flowed from the negative cathode to the positive anode. As the current moved from negative to positive, the radio signal's oscillations were rectified into a detectable direct current. Flemming called this vacuum tube the Thermionic Valve, patenting it in 1905. Later he became a popular lecturer at Cambridge and a consultant to the Edison Electric Light Company; he was knighted in 1929. Earlier, in 1906, the American Lee de Forest added a third electrode – the control grid – to Flemming's valve, creating the triode, a three element valve. Here the low level radio signal was connected to the grid, which then exerted a regulating effect on the flow of electrons from cathode to anode. The result at the anode was an amplification of the grid signal. Triode amplified radios, with diode detector stages, subsequently became commonplace.

EARTH RETURN TELEGRAPHY

Because it relied upon the earth as a "return" conductor, only one wire was necessary for telegraphic transmission. In films of the Wild West, you frequently see single conductors on poles laid alongside the railway track – that is earth return telegraphy.

At the sending end of the link, which could be over several hundred miles from the receiver, one side of a battery (+ve) would be earthed via a good earth connection (cold water pipe) and the other (-ve) side connected to a Morse Key. A single open wire copper line on poles, or underground cable, was in turn connected to earth via a telegraph receiver. When the Morse Key was closed, current flowed from the -ve of the battery, through the key, down the line and through the receiver at the other end to earth, thus completing the circuit. The needle of the receiver would deflect to indicate the presence of a signal.

in the UK throughout the war.

In 1915 Trench Sets were introduced on the Western Front. They were not a great success mainly because they used "earth return" telegraphy and the enemy could easily overhear the messages which were being sent. In more mobile theatres of war, however, where it was less practical to use telegraph and telephone, wireless proved a useful means of communication.

The Post Office Rifles

The formation of a rifle corps at the General Post Office in London was given official approval by the War Office on 13 February 1868. They were designated the 49th Middlesex, and the original Corps consisted of seven companies, entirely recruited from the junior ranks of the Post Office. Senior members were already serving as part of 21 (Civil Service) Corps.

'A Company was formed by staff of the East Central District

'B' Company was formed by staff of the Inland Office

'C' Company was formed by staff of the Newspaper and Money Order offices

'D' Company was formed by staff of the West Central District

'E' Company was formed by staff of the West, South West and South Districts

'F' Company was formed by staff of the North and North West Districts

'G' Company was formed by staff of the East and South East Districts

In June 1869, a new 'H' Company was formed by the South West District, followed in July 1870 by 'I' Company raised by the Telegraph Branch. By the end of 1876, sufficient numbers had been attracted by the East and South East Districts to form separate companies and from January 1877 'G' Company was recruited from East District only, while the men from the South East provided the new 'K' company

The 49th Middlesex was redesignated the 24th in September 1880 and in the following year the corps became one of the volunteer battalions allotted to the Rifle Brigade.

In July 1882 the War Office approved a scheme submitted by the 24th Corps for the formation of an Army Postal Corps. The Corps would undertake all the postal duties connected with an army on active service overseas. It would consist of two officers and 100 men, all recruited from 24th Corps. Two officers and fifty men were to serve overseas while the remainder stayed at home as part of the Army Reserve. Within a short time nearly all of the officers and 350 of the men had volunteered their services and on 8 August 1882 the detachment embarked to join the expeditionary force then in Egypt.

In 1883 recruitment into the telegraph company was stepped up to 200. It was then divided into two divisions 'A' and 'B' and shown in the Army List as 'Field Telegraph Companies'. The following year, the formation of a Field Telegraph Corps was authorised, to be run on the same lines as the Army Post Office Corps. The Corps was to consist of fifty rank and file and after it was formed, it was added to the reserve strength of the Royal Engineers.

In 1889 both the Army Post Office Corps and the Field Telegraph Company were constituted as companies of the 24th Corps. The former provided 'M' Company while the telegraph personnel formed 'L'.

More companies were raised during the Boer War period and in 1908 the 24th Corps became the 8th (City of London) Battalion, the London Regiment (Post Office Rifles).

During World War One, the 8th Battalion won the following battle honours:

1/8 Bn: Festubert, Loos

1/8 Bn:Vimy Ridge, High Wood, Warlencourt

1/8 Bn:Ypres, Messines, Bourlon Wood: 2/8 Bn: Bullecourt, Gravenstaefel, Passchendaele

8 Bn: Tergnier, Villers Bretonneux, Malard Wood, Maricourt, Epehy, Lens, Roeux

Between the First and Second World Wars, the 8th (City of London) Battalion amalgamated with the 7th Battalion and until 1935 remained known as Post Office Rifles. By the outbreak of War, the 7th Battalion had been redesignated The Searchlight Regiment Royal Artillery and during the Second World War was involved in the Air Defence of Britain.

Since 1945, the shape and strength of the Territorial Army has undergone almost continuous change. The name Post Office Rifles has long gone, but members of the Post Office and ancestors of those early Rifle Volunteers no doubt still play a part in Britain's 'Terriers'.

Communication with ships at sea

At the outbreak of World War One, the German communication network was more efficient worldwide than the British. The decision was therefore taken to destroy it. German cables passing through the Channel were cut, in co-operation with the GPO, on 5 August 1914. Allied naval forces also destroyed German wireless stations either by gunfire, as at Dar-es-Salaam and Yap in the Caroline Islands, or by landing troops as at Kamina in Togoland and at Rabaul. Germany's wireless network was therefore of little value to their navy.

British naval communications were far from perfect. Outside home waters and the Mediterranean they depended on cables and a few wireless stations at naval bases. The Germans attempted to attack the cable system: the *Nurnberg* cut the transpacific cable at Fanning Island on 7 September and the *Emden* was in the process of severing the cables at Cocos Island when she was caught by HMAS Sydney. The *Emden*'s presence had been reported by the wire-

Taken during the battle of the Canal du Nord on 27 September 1918, this photograph shows two Artillery Signallers with a Lucas signalling lamp on the bank of the canal near Moeuvres

less station, and the signal was picked up by HMS *Minotaur*, escorting an Australian troop convoy, from which HMAS *Sydney* was despatched to destroy the raider.

The cable system was in fact maintained intact throughout the war, kept in working order by 47 cable ships, 37 of which were British. Cable communication could only contact ships in harbour; the control of ships at sea in general had to be maintained by direct wireless messages from ship to ship. On occasion linking ships had to be used to extend wireless communication, although those using the powerful Mark I set could communicate as far as 2,500 miles (4,000kms) apart. The spark transmitters which still sent their messages over a comparatively wide band of frequencies, coupled with the use of broadly tuned receivers, were mainly responsible.

The system did have one great disadvantage – messages could be picked up by the enemy; jamming was attempted on occasion by both sides, but not very successfully.

In home waters, in 1914, the British wireless network was much as it had been when established in 1909. The main change in 1915 was the establishment of 16 new 'Auxiliary' wireless stations around the British coast and in Ireland.

The British Naval Wireless Instructions of 1915 list 28 different frequencies in use. Long waves were used by shore stations; shorter waves by ships. A stroke of good fortune was the achievement early on in 1914 of breaking the German naval ciphers. At the end of 1914 more high-powered wireless stations were built to cover the main world trade routes. All were for communication with ships; few stations could talk to each other, and their contact with the Admiralty was by cable. Most were in operation by June 1915.

Communications were still further improved by the completion of the high-power Imperial Wireless scheme station at Abu Zaabal in Egypt, and others in Australia and New Zealand.

Another British problem was lack of communication with submarines; their

By World War One, cable was used not only for telegraphy but also for telephone communications. This illustration of Scottish Signal Company, Royal Engineers, going into action was later used as a model for the bronze centrepiece cast by Garrards, the Crown Jewellers, to mark the 75th Anniversary of the Royal Corps of Signals

1Kw transmitters could not be heard by English stations. A submerged submarine could neither receive nor send signals; they were useless as watchdogs on the movements of the High Seas Fleet.

In February 1915 Naval Intelligence began to set up a series of five stations covering the North Sea, using the Marconi Company system of wireless direction finding. These gave warning of seven sorties by the High Seas fleet, and in five of these the alerted Grand Fleet put to sea in an effort to force an action, but without success.

During the first eighteen months of the war, the spark transmitter and crystal receiver proved satisfactory in Home waters. But longer ranges were needed on the oceans. By the end of 1915 the Royal Navy had 35 different types of transmitter and 28 receivers. From 1914-15 wireless and to a certain extent cables dominated the scene. In the following year, the fitting of British patrol submarines with the new 3Kw arc transmitter meant they could now report their sightings to the Admiralty. For the remainder of the war, the main system of naval wireless communication did not greatly alter.

Throughout the war, the telegraph cable was of exceptional value, messages being incapable of interception. Wireless telegraphy, on the other hand, had the great advantage that it could contact ships at sea and broadcast messages to a large number of stations simultaneously. Wireless was of very great value for controlling naval forces at sea, and obtaining intelligence. While it did not produce a new dimension in maritime warfare, it made conventional methods considerably more effective.

The beginnings of Air Defence

Introduction

The principal role of the GPO in World War One was to provide telephone and telegraph communications to support UK air defence. The development of an effective air defence was a slow process, principally due to the lack of a dedicated central control. There was no RAF until April 1918; men and what the Chief of General Staff, Lord Robertson, still referred to as "machines" were under the control of both the Army and the Royal Navy. The result was a constant tug of war between the Western Front and the Home Front for a larger share of these already scarce resources.

The Zeppelin airship changed the nature of warfare at the beginning of the century. For the first time, the civilian population was subjected to direct threat from the enemy.

The principal role of the RFC was to provide offensive and reconnaissance support to the army and navy. Little thought was given to the need to provide Home Air Defence.

This map and that on the next page show the dramatic increase in airpower between 1914 and 1918

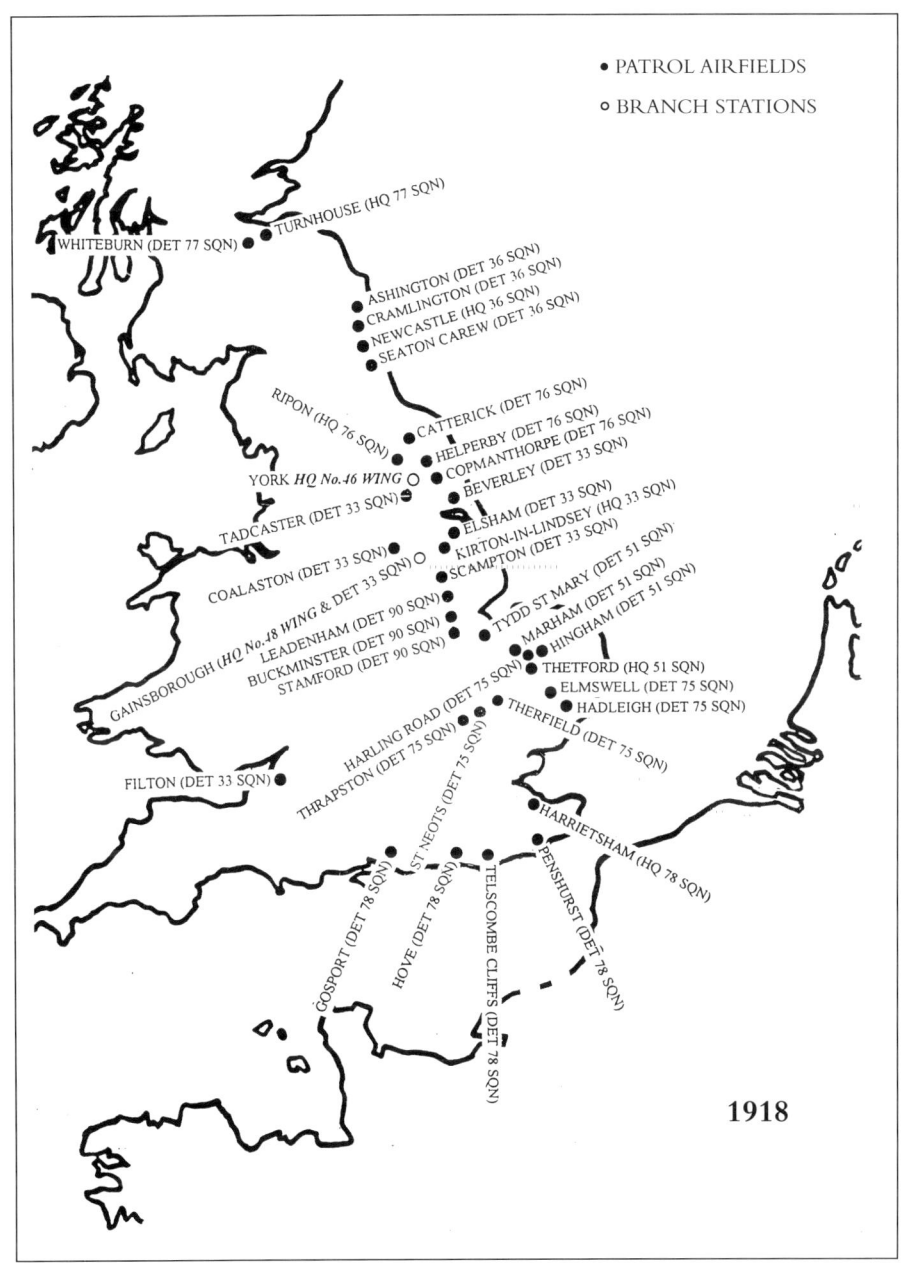

PATROL AIRFIELDS
BRANCH STATIONS

WHITEBURN (DET 77 SQN)
TURNHOUSE (HQ 77 SQN)
ASHINGTON (DET 36 SQN)
CRAMLINGTON (DET 36 SQN)
NEWCASTLE (HQ 36 SQN)
SEATON CAREW (DET 36 SQN)
RIPON (HQ 76 SQN)
CATTERICK (DET 76 SQN)
HELPERBY (DET 76 SQN)
COPMANTHORPE (DET 76 SQN)
YORK HQ No.46 WING
BEVERLEY (DET 33 SQN)
TADCASTER (DET 33 SQN)
ELSHAM (DET 33 SQN)
KIRTON-IN-LINDSEY (HQ 33 SQN)
COALASTON (DET 33 SQN)
SCAMPTON (DET 33 SQN)
GAINSBOROUGH (HQ No.48 WING & DET 33 SQN)
LEADENHAM (DET 90 SQN)
TYDD ST MARY (DET 51 SQN)
MARHAM (DET 51 SQN)
BUCKMINSTER (DET 90 SQN)
HINGHAM (DET 51 SQN)
STAMFORD (DET 90 SQN)
THETFORD (HQ 51 SQN)
ELMSWELL (DET 75 SQN)
HARLING ROAD (DET 75 SQN)
HADLEIGH (DET 75 SQN)
THERFIELD (DET 75 SQN)
FILTON (DET 33 SQN)
THRAPSTON (DET 75 SQN)
HARRIETSHAM (HQ 78 SQN)
ST NEOTS (DET 75 SQN)
GOSPORT (DET 78 SQN)
HOVE (DET 78 SQN)
TELSCOMBE CLIFFS (DET 78 SQN)
PENSHURST (DET 78 SQN)

1918

On the outbreak of War in August 1914 the RFC's military wing was made responsible for air defence of the inland areas of the UK, with the Naval Wing being tasked with the defence of ports, docks and other naval installations. Disagreements between the Admiralty and the War Office led to the break up of the RFC in the summer of 1914. The Naval Wing was brought back under Admiralty control as the Royal Naval Air Service (RNAS) and the Military Wing which retained the title of RFC was restored to the War Office. This was only the beginning of a period of near fatal indecisiveness.

The first planes to drop bombs on British soil were two seaplanes of the German Navy, Friedrichshafen FF29s. Neither did much damage but more attention was paid to London's defence as a result and protective patrol lines were established. They ran from Grimsby in the East and Dungeness in the South to London, and flying stations were established along them. They were given direct GPO telephone links between them, the Admiralty, anti-aircraft batteries and the police. It was hoped that this would give the defenders enough time to get airborne.

The Zeppelin was an almost mystical menace to the public; many reported imaginary sightings but bombing had been ruled out by the Kaiser because 'he did not wish to bomb the country whose King was his cousin'. Later he limited the Navy to attacks on the London Docks, military installations in the lower Thames and along the English Coast. He always excluded the historic areas of London and the royal residences.

The first Zeppelin raid took place on the night of 19 and 20 January 1915 when three Zeppelins dropped bombs on Norfolk, killing four people and injuring a further sixteen. They caused damage to the value of £7,740 (£233,749 in today's prices).

Between May 1915 and January 1916, responsibility for home air defence continued to be passed from the RFC to the RNAS and back again with fatal results. Zeppelin raids increased. Citizens were killed and thousands of pounds worth of damage was being incurred. Dozens of sorties were flown with no effective result.

After the raids in January 1916 the public became even more alarmed. There were reports of massed Zeppelins flying over towns when there were no Zeppelins flying at all. Field Marshal Lord French, GOC Home Forces, quickly instituted the means to provide a proper early warning system which would prevent 'Phantom Zeppelin' scares, and Lieutenant Colonel Philip Maud was given the responsibility of establishing a system of reporting based on telephonic communication.

England, Wales and part of Scotland were divided into eight warning control areas. Each had a controller representing GHQ Home Forces who was responsible for passing on information and issuing warnings. Every area was sub-divided into numbered warning districts, each about 35 square miles (90 sq km) in area.

Assuming the average speed of the enemy airships to be 60 mph (96 kph), it would take about half an hour to cross each district. Each district would be warned in succession and need only put final precautions into effect when the danger was near.

The Warning Controller relied for his information on the extensive cordons of observer posts who relayed information about enemy movements. In turn the Controller told GHQ Home Forces, the Home Defence Squadrons, anti-aircraft stations and the adjacent Controller.

To avoid confusion of identification, every airship which was 'followed' was given a temporary code name to which every unit referred while the raider was over England. Girls christian names were reserved for naval ships, while military airships were given boys names.

Once the Warning Controller had been told where the raiders were, he telephoned the local GPO Engineer-in-Charge who would in turn contact individual subscribers on his 'warning' list. Priority was given to industrial complexes and military authorities who had to take preliminary precautions.

Everyone on the warning list was obliged by law to answer a warning call at any time of the day or night, within fifteen seconds. If there was no reply, the telephone operator passed to the next name on the list but when all calls were completed, he tried again to call those who had not answered. Those who failed to answer were prosecuted, but this was rare as all those who had to take action against an air-raid were fully aware how important it was to see that the system worked.

There were fall-back options in case the GPO system failed or if Zeppelins attacked a town where no previous warnings had been issued. The Police could also issue warnings and so could the military in coastal areas where attacks might materialise suddenly, giving the Warning Controller too little time.

It took a while before the public recognised the warnings for what they were. Initially, civilians rushed outside to look at this new spectacle of bursting shells and sweeping searchlights. In some provincial towns, public warning systems were abandoned. In October 1915, Hull's Chief Constable said that he would not have introduced a buzzer if he had known the effect it would have.

Nevertheless, a system of public warning was in place by March 1916 where local conditions were thought to need it. Three months later, churches, theatres and other public places were placed on the warning list, although the orders were not compulsory.

One other thing worried the Home Office. In December 1915 Chief

Carrier pigeons have been used as messengers since the days of the ancient Greeks. During both World Wars the British Army had pigeon sections, with birds bringing messages back from the front line

Constables were advised that the use of church and clock bells be discontinued between sunset and sunrise, especially in coastal areas. A new regulation was imposed in March 1916 prohibiting the ringing of bells or striking of clocks which might be 'audible at such a distance as to be capable of serving as a guide for hostile aircraft'.

By August 1916 there was beginning to be a public outcry at the lack of an effective air defence. In September, the Admiralty Sub-Committee on Home Defence Flying recommended that defence should concentrate on guns and searchlights rather than aircraft.

In November 1915, not before time, the Admiralty held a conference to discuss whether aeroplanes were essential for the defence of London. Once again the issues were fudged. The Army and Navy agreed that there should be a unified command structure but could not agree on how it should operate.

At long last, in February 1916, the total responsibility for air defence was passed to the War Office. They decided that the Navy should defend the seaward approaches and the RFC the inland areas.

In spite of the more unified approach to air defence, the success rate was still disastrous. On the night of 31 January 1916 came the biggest raid of the war on a number of Midland towns. The defence disaster was put down to lack of night flying

During World War One, dogs as well as pigeons were trained to carry messages between trenches. They also learned to lay cables in conditions where it would have been impossible fro signallers to operate; one is shown here with a small cable drum on his back, held in place by a harness

experience on the part of aircrews, insufficiently robust aircraft construction and a poor reporting and tracking system. At this time the Maud system, previously described had yet to be implemented.

Even then, the continuing pressures from the war in Europe eroded plans for a more effective home defence. The dedicated night-fighter squadrons were formed into a home defence wing. By the late summer of 1916 the ground based early warning system was in place. Improvements in the performance and numbers of night fighters and the quality of the pilots resulted in the neutralisation of the Zeppelin force when four were shot down in flames during the autumn.

By Spring 1917, the vulnerable Zeppelin Force was beginning to be overtaken by newer technology and airships were being replaced by large bombing aeroplanes. However, the Western Front and the increasing U-boat menace were robbing the Home defence of more and more guns and trained pilots. On 6 and 7 May 1917 came the first bombing raid on London by an aeroplane.

Home Defence was taken by surprise when 22 large Gotha bombers appeared over Folkestone, flying in formation to minimise the danger of fighter attacks. Considerable damage was caused; 95 people were killed and some 200 injured.

Although three of the Gothas were destroyed, there was an immediate public outcry at the ease with which the attack took place.

The beginnings of air to ground communication

The increase in speed of the Gothas over the Zeppelins required the warning time prior to an attack to be reduced. The air defence aircraft needed to take off earlier and ideally communications were required from the ground to the pilots.

The Director-General of Aeronautics, Sir David Henderson, called for the development of airborne radio telephony to be speeded up, so that raid reports could be passed to planes already in the air on patrol. However, once again inter-service rivalry came into play, and this call was opposed by the Admiralty, who wanted priority efforts put into solving their own communications problems. The only stop-gap result at this stage was that a small force of anti-aircraft spotters was recalled from France, but it proved totally inadequate.

On 13 June the Gothas returned. They flew up the Thames and bombed London virtually unopposed. Seventy-two bombs were dropped, killing 162 people and injuring over 400.

They had come and gone before British fighters could locate them. The real enemy was time, as the CIGS rightly pinpointed when he said "The distance in time from the Kent coast to important places like London is less than the time required by most of our present machines to ascend to the necessary height". Following a similar raid in July, he added "I am inclined to think that we need a separate air service".

On 11 July, in response to increased public clamour at the lack of effective defence, British Prime Minister Lloyd George appointed a Committee on Air Organisation and Home Defence against Air Raids. The Chairman was General Jan Christian Smuts, former Boer adversary and a dynamic organiser. Between them, he and Sir David Henderson were chiefly responsible for creating the RAF as a separate service. Lord Trenchard, often credited with this, wrote later that 'Henderson had twice the insight and understanding that I had'.

The Committee set up the London Air Defence Area (LADA), which Brigadier-General Ashmore was appointed to command. It was an inspired choice; he was a co-ordinator of genius. GPO engineers were called on to lay telephone lines linking listening posts at local operations centres to LADA Headquarters, and the Headquarters in turn to the individual airfields.

Ashmore was able to complete the work started by Maud and establish an integrated Air Defence scheme of ground observation, intelligence, air defence fighters and good communications with direct links to the fighters both on the ground and in the air.

Air to ground communication

Command and control of the LADA was exercised through the Spring Gardens Air Defence Centre near Admiralty Arch. It provided the co-ordinating link between the ground reporting network, the command and control structure and the night fighters.

Inside the Centre a map table manned by ten plotters showed the whole area. Above was a dais for the senior officers and operational controllers. Information was fed to the plotters via headsets which were connected by landlines to 26 sub-control centres; they in turn got their information from the many observation posts, sound locators and gun and searchlight sites. The plotters moved discs representing individual enemy aircraft observed; rectangles denoted formations. Arrows were used to show the direction of aircraft and formations while defending aircraft were indicated by aircraft-like shapes. A switchboard enabled the LADA Commander to break into the plotters' telephone lines to make direct enquiries. There were also direct lines to the fighter wings. It was confidently stated that the new centre could provide a warning of enemy aircraft within 30 seconds of them being seen, compared to three or more minutes in September 1917.

This major, though long-delayed, advance in ground to air telephony meant that, with the exception of radar, by the end of World War One Britain's air defence organisation was equivalent to that of 1940. The operations and filter rooms of World War Two would have been instantly recognisable to a plotter at the Spring Gardens Air Defence Centre of 1918.

At the end of the war, Great Britain possessed the most advanced Air Defence scheme in the world. It relied heavily on the communications networks provided by the GPO.

BETWEEN THE WARS

Introduction

Between the Armistice and the mid-thirties, little actual progress was made in the improvement of air defence. By 1918 Britain was physically and mentally exhausted, politically disillusioned, and desperately short of funds. Germany had been defeated – most thought permanently – and no-one wanted to look into the future too closely. Treasury economy was the watchword, and in the cuts made by the Geddes financial axe of 1920-22, RAF squadrons were reduced from 188 to 25; airfields from 700 to 100; and personnel from 291,000 to just under 30,000.

By the end of World War One, those responsible for the country's air defence had not only identified most future problems, but had also some idea of the answers, or at least how to discover those answers. The main unresolved problem, already exercising the minds of the nation's leading scientists and engineers, was how to provide sufficiently early warning of future air attacks.

The RAF was established as the third Service on 1 April 1918. However, once the Armistice was signed, and before the year was out, there was talk of disbandment. What stopped that happening was the fact that home defence had been officially designated as a future planning requirement, and the defence of Britain from air attack was now the main responsibility of the RAF.

Their existence as a separate Service was undoubtedly threatened. Fortunately, in addition to their usefulness at home, they were saved by episodes such as the Chanak incident of 1918, when the RAF came to the rescue of a British garrison under siege in Turkey, so proving their worth in overseas policing operations.

But even so, the light blue line was very thinly stretched. At one time a single squadron of Sopwith Snipes, No. 25, constituted the entire UK Home Defence Force of aircraft. Bonar Law, Prime Minister of the new Conservative government in 1922, was in favour of abolishing the RAF, but was persuaded against it by the Salisbury Committee. That summer he resigned; his successor Stanley Baldwin implemented all the Salisbury recommendations. These included increasing the Home Defence Forces from eighteen squadrons to 52 as quickly as possible.

Earlier in 1922 the Government had considered a preliminary scheme, known as the Steel-Bartholomew Plan, for a limited expansion of the RAF to 23 squadrons and the setting-up of sound-locators on the coast to warn of approaching enemy aircraft, with behind them rings of artillery batteries in designated areas to protect London. But this 23-Squadron Plan was quickly superseded by the Salisbury Committee's 52-Squadron Plan.

Yet even with all this planning, the reality was that by the end of 1924 only ten home-based squadrons existed. Their bases were sited north, south and east of London, as well as in Oxfordshire, Gloucestershire and the Salisbury Plain area, as the chief potential air threat of the future was seen as more likely to come from France than a defeated Germany.

Also with France in mind, it was decided to maintain parity with her air force, so the 52 British squadrons would deploy some 400 bombers and 200 fighters; Secretary of State for Air Sir Samuel Hoare estimated that 1928 would be the earliest possible completion date for this ambitious scheme.

Added urgency was provided in 1924 by the energetic Romer Committee, a joint War Office and Air Ministry sub-committee named after Major General Romer who chaired it. The Committee was set up to progress the 52-Squadron Scheme, and to draft a scheme of command measures to alert the defences of approaching raids and the necessary communications for a defensive system. By late 1925 half the 52 squadrons had been formed, which incidentally ensured the survival of the British aircraft industry. The Romer Committee adopted much of the abortive Steel-Bartholomew plan, including dividing the country into sectors and retaining the concept of artillery zones. But progress was slow; between 1925 and 1928 only six more squadrons were added and by 1932, nine years after the plan was launched, it was still ten short of the 52-squadron target, while backup on the ground was still extremely inadequate.

Meanwhile the growing menace from Nazi Germany was becoming increasingly evident, and in 1934 it was decided that the RAF should again be expanded. This time the British air defence was re-orientated away from France and towards Germany, taking into account the increasing range of bombers, as planned by the Brooke-Popham Re-Orientation Committee in 1935. Fighter squadrons were to be increased from seventeen to 25; there were also to be more artillery and searchlight batteries, and observer posts. In the following year, Bomber Command and Fighter Command were set up as separate entities, with Air Chief Marshal Sir Hugh Dowding as the first C-in-C of the latter.

The advance alerting and mobilising of air defences was the main remaining problem. It was to be solved by radar, whose rapid development is described later in this chapter.

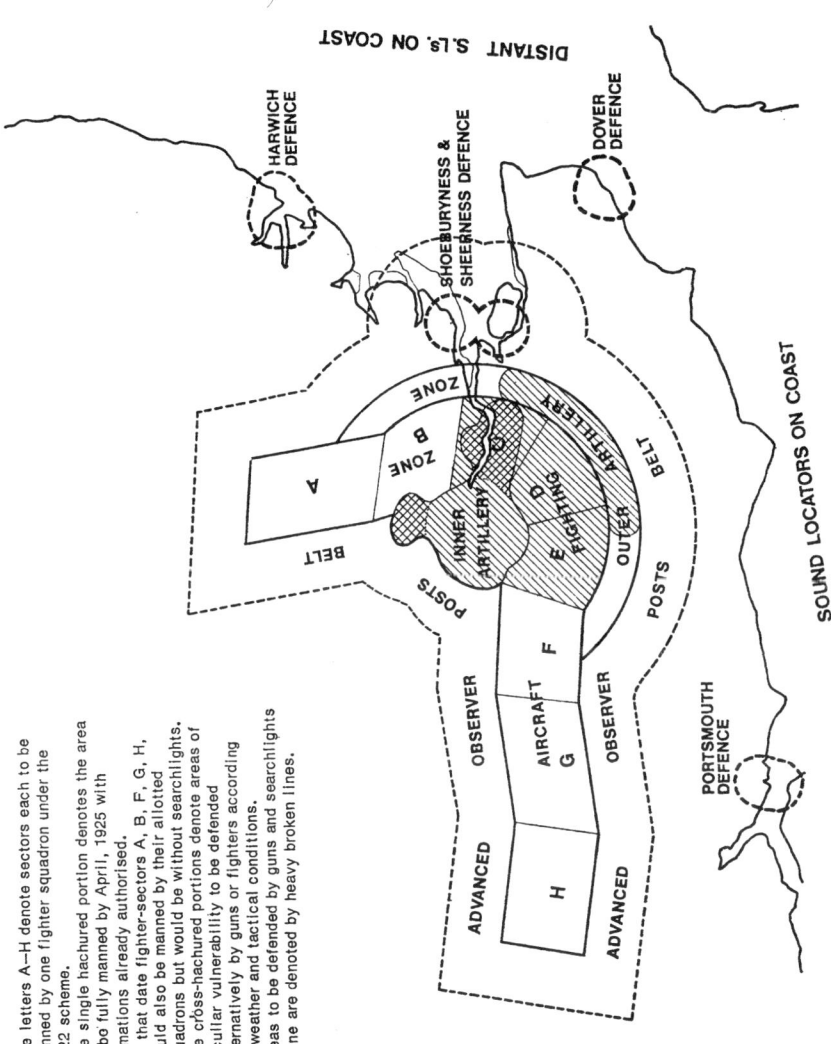

The letters A–H denote sectors each to be manned by one fighter squadron under the 1922 scheme.

The single hachured portion denotes the area to be fully manned by April, 1925 with formations already authorised.

By that date fighter-sectors A, B, F, G, H, would also be manned by their allotted squadrons but would be without searchlights. The cross-hachured portions denote areas of peculiar vulnerability to be defended alternatively by guns or fighters according to weather and tactical conditions.

Areas to be defended by guns and searchlights alone are denoted by heavy broken lines.

The Steel-Bartholomew Plan (1923)

59

AUTOMATIC TELEPHONE SWITCHING

Interconnecting subscribers by verbal instructions and manual connections required thousands of operators. It was time-consuming, costly and inevitably inefficient.

Automatic exchanges were the answer. Just three years after Alexander Graham Bell invented the telephone in 1876, the first patent for such an exchange was granted in the US. The next decade saw other systems patented, but they were impractical or had limitations.

In 1891, Alamon B Strowger of Kansas City patented the basic principle of the two-motion telephone selector. His device required five wires from the subscriber to the exchange, later reduced to two with the introduction of relay controlled signalling.

Strowger's principles were adopted as standard in both the US and the UK. His switch comprised a shaft with a set of wipers that climbed vertically and then rotated horizontally under the control of digits generated by a subscriber's dial. During the horizontal motion the wipers made contact with a number of copper outlets before stopping on the desired one. Each switch had ten vertical levels and ten horizontal outlets, controlling calls between blocks of 100 subscribers. Ringing current was extended automatically by relay controlled testing circuits. For automatic working, subscriber telephones had to be replaced by one with a ten pulses per second rotary dial.

The first public automatic exchange was opened in the US in 1892, followed over the next decade by 20 to 30 different types. The UK's first automatic exchange was demonstrated in 1897, but the first fully operational exchange was not opened by the GPO until 1912 at Epsom,. Surrey.

World War One retarded the development and implementation of automatic telephony, but the post-war period provided a new impetus. The trunk network was automated, as by 1939 were many local urban exchanges. In that year the public UK network comprised 3,250,000 telephones generating 2,236mn calls annually. During World War Two, traffic increased considerably; by 1949 the GPO operated 5,848 local exchanges of which 4,000 were automatic, and these generated 3,137mn annual calls - approximately nine million per day. By 1964, 70 per cent of all UK subscribers were connected to automatic exchanges.

Landline communications and the establishment
of the Air Defence Force

Soon after the end of World War One, the Air Ministry asked the GPO to provide the landlines and telephone exchanges which they needed. The GPO had already carried out similar work for the War Office. The RAF accepted the responsibility of providing wireless communications.

Landline communications for the air and ground units which made up the Home Defence Force were an integral part of the Home Defence Scheme approved by the Government in 1923. The recommended landline systems included:

- A line communication system between the Observation Posts and Observation Centres of the Observer Corps to Fighting Area HQ.

- A line telephone system connecting coastguard stations with Observation Centres.

- A line telephone system between aircraft sectors, searchlight batteries, anti-aircraft gun groups, etc.

- A line telephone system linking the Air Officer Commanding – AOC – Fighting Area with all HQ and formations under his command during operations and also with defended areas on the coast.

- A line telephone system linking the Service Commanders with all Government Departments, Fighting Area Headquarters and bombing formations.

Each Service was to be responsible for the provision and maintenance of the circuits required. The Army was also at that time responsible for the communications needed by the Observer Corps; this responsibility was transferred to the RAF in 1928. In the event of war, overall control would be taken by the Army. If an expeditionary force was dispatched, the lines, signals offices and telephone exchanges would be provided and run by the Army Signal Service.

The Romer Committee gave the task of working out a complete scheme of landline communications for the air defence of Great Britain to the Air Officer Commander in Chief (AOC-in-C), Air Defence of Great Britain. He formed an Air Defence Landline Telephones Committee for the purpose.

John Ellington had been a Major on the staff of the GOC Air Defence Formation of the Territorial Army for just over a year when he was asked to become a member of the Air Defence Landline Telephones Committee. Other committee mem-

---

THE OBSERVER CORPS

The Observer Corps was officially established following the approval of the Committee of Imperial Defence on 29 October 1925, although the idea and the inspiration which promoted the foundation of the Corps belongs to much earlier times.

The Observer Corps provided the "eyes and ears" of the RAF. The land area of the country was divided into a number of Observer Areas which were themselves divided into Observer Groups. Each Group had an Observer Centre sited in or just outside a main town near or next to a telephone exchange.

Observer Posts situated some six to ten miles apart sent to these centres reports of all aircraft flying. The Posts, usually in clusters of three, reported to plotters sitting round the operations table in the Observer Centre. Each Post could hear what was being reported by its fellow posts in the cluster and the sum of their information was plotted on the operations table.

The Observer Centre thus acted as a "post office" where all the information was collected, sorted and filtered and sent to the right recipient.

"Tellers", seated in a position where they could overlook the operations table, passed the information to RAF Sectors and Groups. At the beginning of the war, it was sent upwards to Fighter Command from the Fighter Group Operations Rooms by "Command Tellers". Later with the introduction of a teleprinter system (eventually discarded in 1943) and a multiphone broadcast, the whole system was simplified, though speech telling was retained as a standby and was used during breakdowns of the main systems.

---

bers were drawn from the staffs of AOC-in-C, the Air Defence Formations of the Territorial Army and finally from the GPO. John lived with his wife and two children in Bywater Street, a stone's throw from Chelsea Barracks, and taught physics at Westminster School. Since a boy he had been fascinated by science and electricity and his service with GOC Air Defence Formation of the Territorial Army enabled him both to keep abreast of the latest developments in communication technology and to put these developments into practice during periods of active service.

The terms of reference for the Committee were no less than to draw up a complete scheme of the landline communications which would eventually be required for the air defence of Great Britain. When the scheme was complete, it had to submitted to the War Office and Air Ministry. When they in turn had agreed the scheme, it was to be lodged with the GPO.

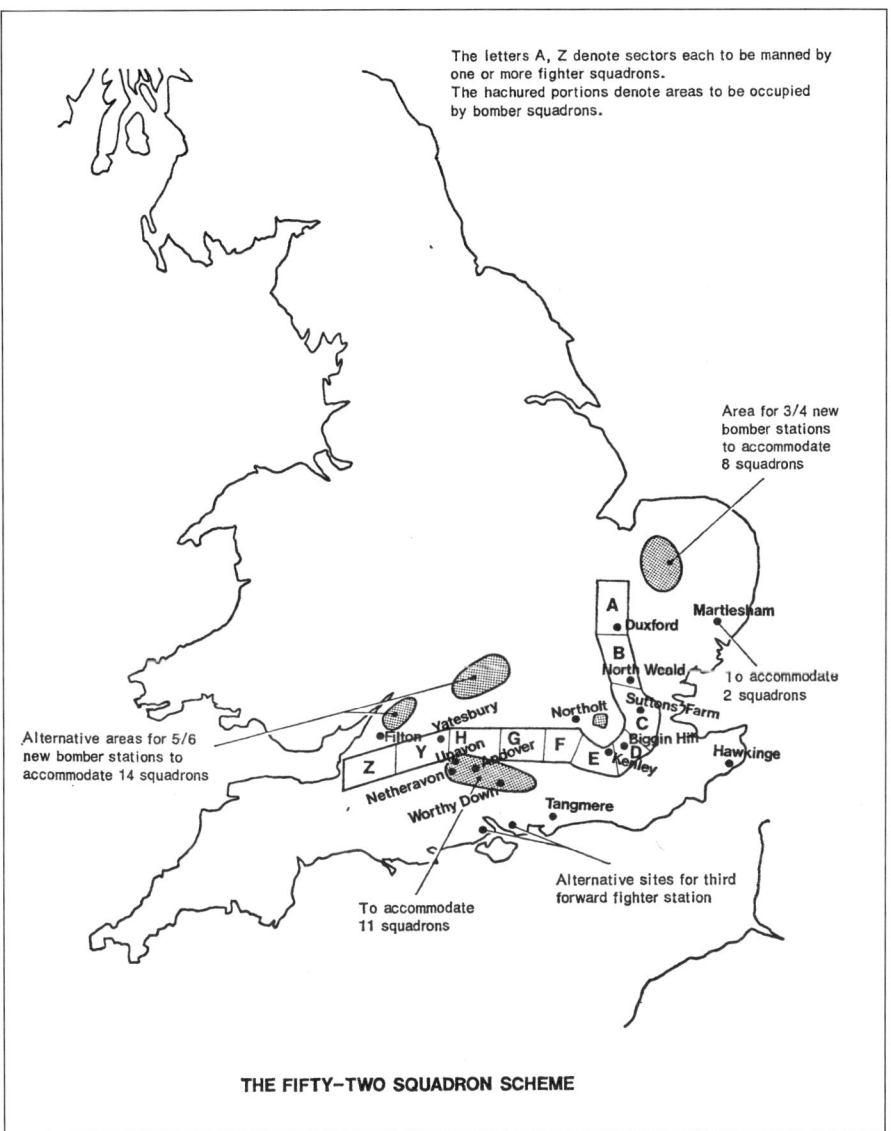

The letters A, Z denote sectors each to be manned by one or more fighter squadrons.
The hachured portions denote areas to be occupied by bomber squadrons.

Area for 3/4 new bomber stations to accommodate 8 squadrons

Martlesham

A
● Duxford

B
● North Weald
● Suttons Farm
Northolt ●
C
● Biggin Hill
Kenley

1 o accommodate 2 squadrons

Hawkinge

Alternative areas for 5/6 new bomber stations to accommodate 14 squadrons

● Filton   ● Yatesbury
Y   Upavon   G
Z   Netheravon   Andover   F
H   Worthy Down   E
D

Tangmere

Alternative sites for third forward fighter station

To accommodate 11 squadrons

THE FIFTY–TWO SQUADRON SCHEME

The Proposal by the Salisbury Committee 1924-5 which was based on the 1923 Steel-Bartholomew Plan

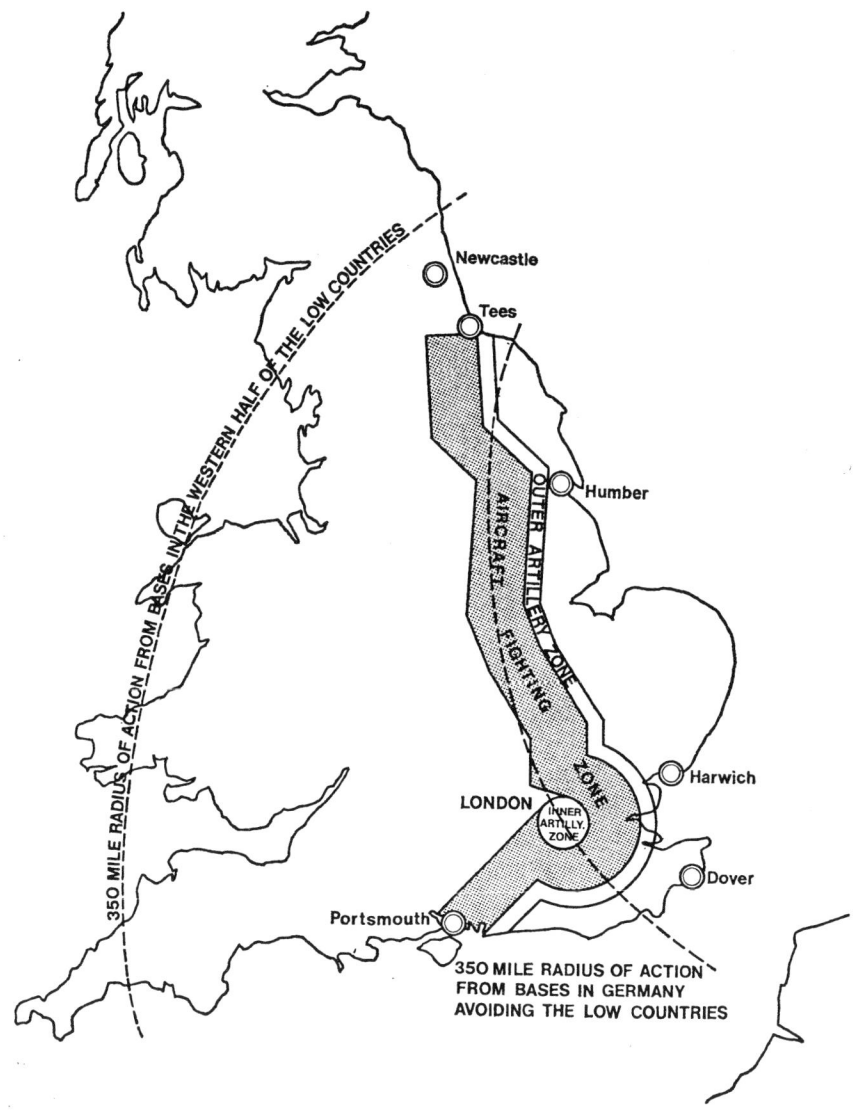

THE REORIENTATION SCHEME (1935)

Meetings of the Committee were mentally demanding and inevitably members found themselves with work and study to do afterwards. But at length the new committee presented the report to the Home Defence Committee where it was classified as "Home Defence Committee Paper No. 90". The report was agreed and the schedule remained the basis of all operational landline requirements for air defence. Nearly a third of the cost was to come from normal telephone development. John returned to his normal teaching duties and part-time soldiering with the TA. However, the work of the committee was not finished. Cabinet policy in 1924 had been based on the assumption that war would not happen for at least ten years and they hoped that by delaying the implementation of the full schedule, the London telephone network – which was expanding fast – would provide quite a number of the circuits specified. Money would be saved.

However, by 1928, it was clear that the work of the committee was being carried out on too narrow a basis and a new committee was established with representatives from both War Office and Air Ministry. Again John was asked to become a member.

This time, instead of a fixed plan, the committee was required to keep continually under review the scheme of landline communications required for the Air Defence of Great Britain. This would take into account any alterations or additions proposed from time to time. Finally, every year until the landline scheme was completed, the committee was to draw up proposals for the telephone communications needed for the air defence training exercises for the following season with an estimate of the cost required.

John remained on the Committee until 1940 when, as a First Line Reserve, he was called up for Active Service with the RAF. His specialised knowledge of communications by that stage gave him a unique status and he served for most of the war as a Group Captain and later Air Commodore at Fighter Command Headquarters at Stanmore.

By 1934, there were still no permanent landlines between RAF Fighter Command at Uxbridge and the sector stations. Temporary arrangements had to be made each year for operational landlines to cover the annual exercises.

A series of Trials in 1935/36 held by the RAF and the GPO determined in detail what the wartime needs of the Fighter Group Operations Room might be. By May 1936, sufficient experience had been gained to prepare a schedule of the lines and circuits required.

The GPO were asked to look into the possibility of routing circuits through the GPO network, bearing in mind the need for three separate routes for survivability purposes. Spare circuits, searchlight circuits and sector requirements were all con-

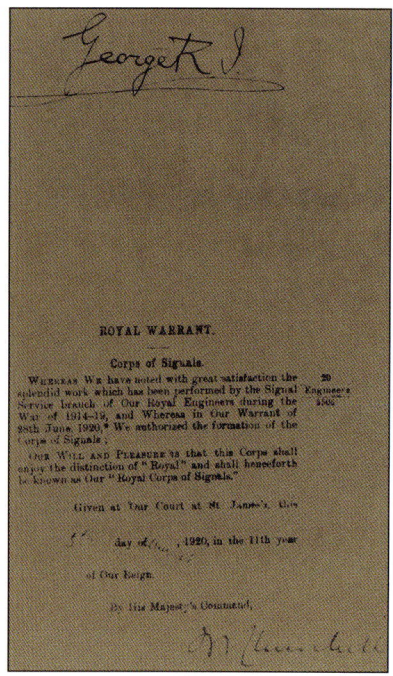

ROYAL WARRANT.

Corps of Signals.

The Royal Warrant of King George V, dated 28 August 1920 and countersigned by Winston Churchill, conferred the title 'Royal' on the Corps of Signals. Recognition of the importance of battle communications had led to the Corps being formed from the RE Signal Service six weeks earlier

sidered. Eventually the Army was made responsible for searchlight circuits between visual plotter stations the local GPO exchange, the RAF accepted responsibility for arranging circuits between the exchanges and the sector operations room. The GPO met all of these needs and in addition allowed for some extra circuits as "spares", bringing the total number up to about 250.

Formation of the Royal Corps of Signals

It had become clear in World War One that communications played such a vital part in modern warfare that a Corps of specialists was needed. Even before Armistice Day in 1919, the War Office was considering the formation of a separate Corps. It was clear that the Signal Service had become a virtually separate entity from the Royal Engineers.

The Royal Warrant establishing the Corps of Signals was issued on 28 June 1920, signed by the then Secretary of State for War, Rt Hon Winston S Churchill. On 5 August, King George V conferred the title Royal on the new Corps. In October of the same year, the Royal Corps of Signals were accorded Army precedence immediately below their parent corps, the Corps of Royal Engineers. Soldiers serving in the Royal Engineers Signals Service were transferred to the new Corps, while most of the officers were seconded from other regiments. From 1924, officers were commissioned directly into the Royal Signals. The figure of Mercury, the Roman Messenger of the Gods, was chosen as the Unit Insignia.

The development of Radar

Research on radar began in earnest following a paper written by Arnold Watkins and presented by Robert Watson-Watt, Superintendent of the Radio Department of the National Physical Laboratory, at the beginning of 1935 to the Committee for Scientific Survey of Air Defence (CSSAD).

The Committee had been considering the possibility of a "death ray" which could destroy aircraft. Watson-Watt's paper showed that it was impractical to produce enough radiated energy for destructive purposes but that detection and location of aircraft at a distance was, in theory, possible.

Following Watson-Watt's paper, the Committee authorised the expenditure of £4,000 on experimental equipment and asked the Treasury for another £10,000. Air Marshal Sir Hugh Dowding, then Air Council Member for Research and Development, would not agree without some form of practical demonstration so in February 1935 an experiment using the continuing wave radiation from the GPO's Daventry Wireless Station and a receiver from the National Physical Laboratory at Weedon was conducted. The equipment successfully detected a Heyford bomber at a distance of about eight miles (thirteen kms).

The Treasury approved expenditure of £12,300, a team of scientists began work at Orfordness on 13 May and by 15 June 1935 had given their first demonstration. By 31 July aircraft were being recorded at 40 miles range (64km). Soon afterwards, nearby Bawdsey Manor was taken over for a second receiver station and from the end of 1935 became the development HQ for radar. This had all happened within a year. In fact, the term 'radar' did not come into use in the UK until 1941. Before that date, it was known as 'radio direction finding', or RDF .

With the coming of radar, the Air Staff began to formulate completely new plans for air defence. These were built around a chain of early-warning stations incorporating radar, the go-ahead for the construction of which had been given in 1935. The stations were known collectively as Chain Home, or CH for short. A chain of 20 was envisaged, and the Air Staff called for seven trial stations to be in place between the Tyne and Southampton in time for the August 1936 air defence exercises.

Squadron Leader Hart and the Biggin Hill experiment

Earlier that same year, Squadron Leader R G Hart was given the task of advising Fighter Command on how to train their personnel to operate CH Radar. He was attached to Bawdsey and appointed Commandant of Radio Direction Finding Training.

Hart quickly found that considerable confusion could result from the double-reporting of enemy aircraft by adjacent radar stations. There was an obvious need for preliminary evaluation to be taken at a lower level, sorting out the sightings correctly before the plots were sent to the operations centres.

His simple but brilliantly effective solution was to introduce Filter Rooms, halfway houses where plots from all the CH stations in a particular sector were displayed and analysed by an experienced controller.

By August 1936, sufficient telephone circuits had been made available for HQ Fighter Command to carry out an exercise at Biggin Hill – one of the chosen Sector

HQs – in order to evaluate Hart's idea.

Although the Biggin Hill controllers were unaware of the source of their information – Radar Defence being still top secret – they successfully directed No 32 Squadron's Gloster Gauntlets onto the raiders simulated by Hawker Harts.

Hart was vindicated; filtering was immediately adopted, and remained the standard part of early-warning procedures until the end of World War Two and beyond into the 1950s. This decision added another level into the air defence organisation that required yet another reconfiguration of the cable network by the GPO.

Chain Home

Following the success of Biggin Hill, and the other tests which were carried out in April of 1937, approval was given by the Treasury to build first five and then 20 Chain Home stations. However, due largely to lack of resources, the project was slow to develop and by mid 1937 Bawdsey, on the Suffolk Coast, was still the only operational station.

It was vital to speed up the work. Industry was brought in to begin the production of equipment. For secrecy, different contractors were used for different parts of the equipment. Metropolitan-Vickers carried out the design and production of the transmitters, A C Cossor did similar work on the receivers, the Radio Transmission Equipment Company worked on goniometers and the aerials were the responsibility of the Bawdsey staff, assisted by the GPO.

In November 1937, 20 sets of equipment were ordered at a total cost of £380,000. By the time of the Munich Crisis in September 1938 the first five stations were completed. They were Bawdsey, Great Bromley, Dover, Dunkirk and Canewdon. The South East corner of England had their radar protection shield in place. This was the beginning of the National CH radar network.

By the outbreak of war in September 1939 a chain of eighteen radar stations was operational and reporting to the Stanmore Filter and two other independent CH stations. Though these ground based chain radars could detect enemy aircraft they were not yet accurate enough to guide fighter planes to a successful interception. Radar interception trials were meanwhile continuing at Bawdsey Research Station but with poor results. The tracking information which was being given to the sector operations room was too erratic and inaccurate for interceptions to be achieved

By this time point to point communication by wireless had been relegated to a standby role, as landline provision by the GPO had advanced to meet the needs of stations in the United Kingdom.

By the outbreak of war, the radar network and the associated GPO communications infrastructure were well advanced and able to support the country's air defences.

WORLD WAR TWO

Introduction.

During World War Two, every gun site, barrage balloon, observer corps post, Home Guard headquarters and civil defence post depended upon the GPO for their efficient operation. RAF Bomber, Fighter and Coastal Command airfields and operations rooms, Army camps and depots and Naval establishments required vast networks of communications in all parts of the country. In addition, there were the communications needs of the Royal Ordnance Factories and Government Departments, made even more complex when they were split up and evacuated to different parts of the country.

Once established, all these communication networks had to be maintained and repaired. Research was needed, too. The GPO examined a variety of problems of a highly technical nature; they frequently resulted in the development of new and varied types of Service equipment.

The GPO undertook the purchase of telecommunication equipment required by the Services abroad, acting for the Supply Ministries and Board of Trade. It also undertook the control of the manufacture and supply of equipment and cable for users in the Dominions, Colonies and Allied forces, cable ships and radio stations; it maintained external communications and was heavily involved in the D-Day arrangements.

Non-telecommunication tasks were also entrusted to the GPO. These included tasks like providing Morrison and Anderson shelters for the Home Office, remote control facilities for illuminating areas where buried people needed to be found and unexploded bombs located. There was barely an aspect of the war in which the GPO did not play a part; communications had never been more important.

There was a strong pacifist and anti-war feeling in Britain after the end of World War One. Drastic cuts were made in army manpower and equipment. As a result, when World War Two broke out the Army was ill equipped. The Royal Signals Unit which went to France with the British Expeditionary Force in 1939 had been quickly expanded in the previous months but some of the men were not fully trained and a lot of the equipment was obsolete.

For a year Europe held its breath. Using the time gained earlier by Chamberlain's prolonged negotiations with Hitler, Britain began slowly to re-arm. Without the period of that 'phoney' war, the outcome could have been very different.

In May 1940 Hitler's assault swept across Western Europe. In turn, Holland, France and Belgium fell. The BEF deployed into Belgium to meet the advance along roads blocked by refugees but it was too small and poorly armed to stem the flood. The English coastal airfields were filled with fighter Squadrons which had been moved forward to intervene but away from their bases, at the limit of their range and without ground control, they suffered heavy losses.

The BEF were obliged to retreat and concentrated in Dunkirk where nearly 400,000 troops awaited rescue. In spite of heavy losses, the RAF provided a protective umbrella over the flotilla of little ships carrying exhausted British troops back to England. The evacuation of 338,000 Allied officers and men from Dunkirk became a legend.

After Dunkirk

After the fall of France in 1940, there were two urgent tasks: to provide anti-invasion communications for the Army and communications for Air Defence.

The importance of telephonic communication was highlighted and new systems were developed. For fortresses and base areas in Britain the Army largely relied on the GPO to install and maintain the telephones. GPO telephone lines were augmented by cables laid by Royal Signals. In addition, a wireless network and carrier pigeons were all made ready in case of an invasion.

Oh for the life of a GPO Engineer!

George Single had lived in Dover all his life. His father had been a Postman and George followed in his footsteps by joining the GPO as a bright lad of 14. By quiet and determined application he used his years of apprenticeship to join the ranks of the engineers, always conspicuous in their small dark-green service vans.

As early as 1925, George had been involved in setting up the special landlines for the RAF; by 1939 he was back in Dover, having seen the strategic network of intercommunication between the Services extended and enlarged until it had approached and was later to exceed that maintained for public use.

When war was declared, George was too old to be called up for active service; but as he said later his wartime service was certainly active. The number of GPO engineers who were absorbed into the armed services reduced the regular staff by nearly 25 per cent and those remaining worked to full capacity and beyond during the war years.

Fortunately, a number of precautionary measures had been taken before the war. Foreseeing the paralysing effect that air raids would have on communications, extra cables had been laid between important towns and over different routes. Locations which were thought to be vulnerable to bombing were by-passed. Old telephone exchanges were not dismantled when newer, automatic exchanges were built, but instead were held in reserve. Public trunk lines were promptly switched over for the use of the Services in September 1939.

Following the Dunkirk evacuation, George saw the thousands of pale and gaunt troops arriving back in Dover. The town remained in the front line throughout the war because German troops occupied the whole of the Pas de Calais and this corner of Kent lay within easy range of bombardment. For more than four years, Dover remained a prime target and had to endure constant air raids and bomb damage.

Do Germans come in 5s?

Maurice Le Marchant was working as a GPO Engineer at the Torquay Telephone Exchange when war broke out. At the time it occupied the upper floors of the main Post Office building.

"Because of my knowledge of transmissions, I was involved in maintaining a small Repeater Station which was added to the Automatic Telephone Exchange. What was significant about it was that it contained the terminals for two hybrid carrier circuits working via Dartmouth and submarine cables to Guernsey and Jersey.

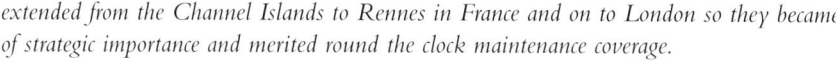

Initially these cables terminated on the Torquay manual switchboard but after war was declared they were extended from the Channel Islands to Rennes in France and on to London so they became of strategic importance and merited round the clock maintenance coverage.

My colleagues and I worked on ten-hour shifts and our favourite shift was from 10pm to 6am. We could turn the lights down low and doze in a deckchair and blanket – unless there was a cable fault in which case you really earned your pay! Very occasionally the Inspector paid a surprise visit, but he was a kind man and always whistled through his teeth as he approached, giving us time to fold our chairs and comb our hair.

For protection, we were issued with a large torch and a huge Colt .45 revolver with 5 cartridges. We always wondered why that number was chosen – did Germans come in fives?

Eventually the Germans occupied most of Europe and as they came west, these lines were the last secure link to France. When they occupied the Channel Islands, the GPO Cable Inspector was on the beach with a hacksaw to sever the link. In fact this turned out to be a mistake and they had to be repaired in order that they could be diverted in mid-channel to link with other cables to New York".

The possible use of poison gas by enemy raiders was an ever-present fear in the early days of World War Two. With this in mind, and to protect their communications lifelines, the Post Office formed their own Gas Decontamination Squad. Members are shown here during practice in Richmond Park, London

The Home Front: Keeping the population informed

In 1940, it was suggested that the population could be warned of an impending enemy invasion by the ringing of church bells. Those whose idea this was appeared to have ignored the fact that churches were not usually on the telephone, bell-ringing was not something which any passer-by could do, and it was highly likely that considerable time might elapse between the alert and the actual ringing of the bells. In

Searchlight drill being carried out by the Searchlight Battalion of the RE 32nd (7th City of London) Anti-Aircraft Battalion. The 7th Battalion had amalgamated with the 8th City of London Battalion and until 1935 remained known as the Post Office Rifles

fact, the system was used only twice – on 7 and 9 September 1940. On both occasions, fortunately, it was a false alarm. After that the sad undulating air raid sirens provided by the GPO proved an excellent and speedy method of warning industry and the general public of impending air raids.

The requirement was for a raid reporting system enabling movements of hostile and friendly aircraft to be plotted on a map in a Service Operations Room, a communication system which could distribute or broadcast air raid warning messages and remote control systems for sounding public warning sirens on receipt of these warnings. The system was under development throughout the war.

Industrial air raid warnings and all-clears were given by bell codes to groups of factories. These warnings indicated a state of imminent danger.

Extensive use was made of the public telephone network for the Public Air Warning system. This could result in delays during the day because it was not possible to differentiate between warning messages and other traffic. At night junctions were set aside to be used as private wires for the sole purpose of passing air raid messages.

Because of the delays which occurred when sending warning messages over the public telephone network, it was essential that this was not compounded by any delay in sounding the sirens after a message was received. The most straightforward system involved the telephone exchange operating staff sounding the sirens from the switch room as soon as they received a message for distribution. The system allowed all sirens up to 30 miles (48 kms) away to be controlled remotely.

In RAF Stations and certain coastal districts, sirens were fitted with a "Cuckoo" attachment which gave a distinctive signal.

The delay between the warning officer initiating the message and the sirens sounding in the London Central District was eventually reduced to about five seconds. To achieve this, all sirens in that district were put under the control of one button in New Scotland Yard and the warning officer at the centre responsible had a private wire to the Yard.

The GPO did much during the war to keep pace with the demands of the Ministry of Home Security for improvements to the system and tribute to their work was paid in 1945 by the Minister in the House of Commons.

Today a national emergency would probably best by conveyed by television's 24 hour news service.

The GPO Circuit Laboratory

The GPO Engineering Department established its Circuit Laboratory in 1924 to design and develop specialised telecommunications equipment.

During World War Two, the Circuit Laboratory was well placed to make a major contribution to the technical war effort by designing, testing and providing telephones and switching facilities using automatic equipment which met the special needs of the Services.

Perhaps most famously, it was used to develop equipment for the RAF, principally the radar station "Fruit Machine" calculators. The calculator was used to convert range and bearing figures from the CH radars into a map grid reference and this was displayed on a panel in front of the operator together with the aircraft height. Many thousands of these were built and deployed to RAF radar stations throughout the war.

At its peak roughly 200 GPO staff were committed to installing and maintaining these machines.

Bernard Brown

Working in the Engineer in Chief's office at the Circuit Laboratory, Bernard Brown was intimately involved in the practical work carried out by the Circuit Laboratory which worked closely with the Air Ministry, the Army and Defence Companies in designing, building and testing the equipment needed for the war effort:

"Two major installations were undertaken by the Circuit Laboratory and I was involved in both of them.

The first was at the Army HQ of the 1st AA Signals set up at the beginning of the war in the disused London Underground station at Brompton Road, Kensington. It became the communication and control centre for all 64 Anti Aircraft gun sites around London.

The old station had three shafts to the station below, each 23 feet across. Two had been lift shafts. The third contained a spiral staircase with 120 steps from street level to the platform which provided the only means of access to the lower levels. There was no water supply below ground so workers at platform level learned to postpone calls of nature as long as possible

One of the former lifts shafts was used to lower heavy equipment and the other was converted into three Gun Operation rooms – GOR 1, 2 and 3, one on top of the other.

At railway level, a wall was built at the side of the track to isolate the tube trains which were still running by. Racks of telephone type signalling and switching equipment were installed along the whole length of the platform and in the first Gun Operation Room (GOR1). An old style modified manual switchboard was also installed across the centre of GOR1 and this was used by the Army Control Officers.

In front of them was a large panel containing 64 smaller display panels, connected to the AA gun sites. When there was aircraft activity in the area of a gun site, data would be keyed in, such as hostile, friendly, bearing, range etc. The Control Officers were able to broadcast this infor-

mation to any of the AA gun sites together with the appropriate action orders.

The Circuit Laboratory work involved installing a large number of multi-wire telephone type cables over the long distances between the apparatus racks on the platform, along passages, stairways and finally up the shaft to the first Gun Operation Room. Installation and testing was completed in December 1939. We remained on site to "dig out the gremlins" and to train two men from the London Telephone Region to take over the responsibility of maintaining the system.

After installing the communication and control centre for the Army at the old Brompton Road Underground Station, Bernard Brown became involved with the much larger project of installing telecommunication equipment in radar stations around the British coast from Land's End to the Orkney and Shetland Islands:

"An early form of electromechanical calculator was designed by the Circuit Laboratory and the Air Ministry and this was commonly known as the "fruit machine". It was our job to instal these calculators at all the Chain Home Stations and connect them to the radar receivers. When an aircraft entered the radar beam from the station transmitter it reflected an echo to the receiver and this was seen on a cathode ray tube, like a television screen. The display showed a horizontal line and the echo could be seen as a blip dipping below the line. The calculator was used to convert range and bearing figures into a map grid reference and this was displayed on a panel in front of the operator together with the aircraft height.

The data was immediately transmitted by telephone to the "filter room" at Fighter Command Stanmore (or other filter rooms in different parts of the country). The speed with which the Radar Stations spotted and fed the plots of enemy aircraft to Fighter Command was an important factor in the winning of the Battle of Britain.

In 1942, the speed was further increased when an Automatic Message Recorder, developed by the Circuit Laboratory, transmitted the information from the radar receiver to the filter rooms at Fighter command stations by teleprinter. We started the Message Recorder installations in the autumn of 1942 at Norwich and continued right round the coast to Sennen at Land's End, completing the task in December 1943.

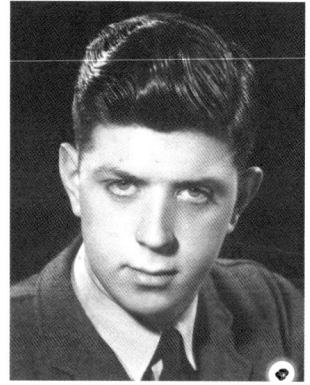

Basil Woods was also involved in this work:

"The small band of GPO engineers who carried out this secret work were often sent to Radar stations in very remote parts of the UK and strong bonds of friendship developed between them. Some of them were later absorbed into the RAF to maintain the equipment while other former GPO Engineering Department employees were later transferred to the RAF from the Royal Corps of Signals.

In 1944 we formed an old colleagues Association called The Fellowship of Apes (not an acronym but a word chosen to *epitomise the unusual antics of members during wartime. The Apes continued to meet every year for the next 50 years; although many of our number have now ended their innings, the friendship of those remaining remains undiminished".*

The Battle of Britain

After Dunkirk, Germany had seemed invincible. First Poland and then the smaller countries of Europe had been occupied and in a matter of weeks most of France had been crushed. Britain's soldiers had lost much of their equipment on the beaches of Dunkirk and had returned in poor shape. When the Germany army had advanced to the very beaches on the other side of the channel, the situation appeared critical.

There followed a lengthy period of fencing during June and July 1940 and by the time the first major offensive by the Luftwaffe took place on 12 August 1940 – the date recognised as being the first day of the Battle of Britain – Air Marshal Sir Hugh Dowding had managed to restore the RAF's position to that which had existed before

The Supermarine Spitfire IIA of Squadron Leader D O Finlay, CO of No 41 Squadron, RAF Hornchurch, in December 1940

Hawker Hurricane I of No 85 Squadron, RAF Debden and Croydon, in August 1940. These revolutionary aircraft inflicted such heavy losses on the Luftwaffe that daylight raids effectively ended on 15 September 1940

the fall of France. Britain's Hurricanes and Spitfires eventually inflicted such heavy losses on the Luftwaffe that the German daylight raids effectively ended on 15 September. Two days later, *Operation Sealion* (Hitler's Invasion Plan for Britain) was abandoned. Occasional daylight raids did continue until October but on a reduced scale as the Luftwaffe switched to night attacks and the targets switched from the RAF to London and the big cities. The work of the GPO in providing telecommunications facilities for Fighter Command had become a vital ingredient in the battle for Britain's skies.

Fighter Command Communications

Great Britain was divided into Sectors by the RAF, each in control of several airfields within its area. The Sectors were grouped together on a regional basis to form Groups. Each Group was responsible to Headquarters Fighter Command. During the

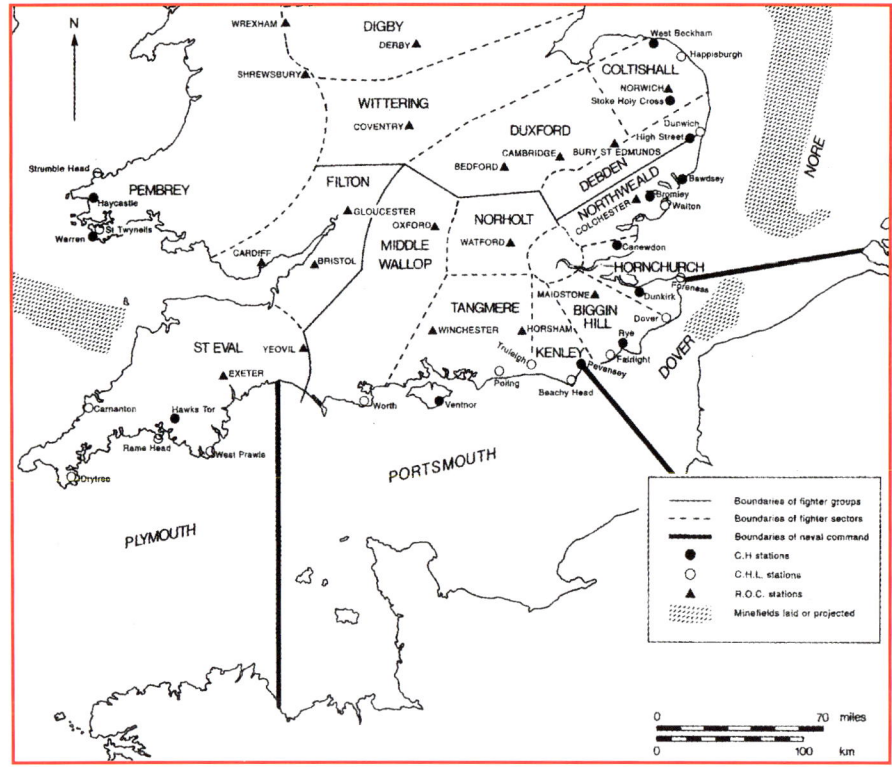

Map of maritime defence, radar chain and fighter sectors, 1940 (After B. Collier 1957)

Battle of Britain, there were 35 Sectors and seven groups which had been connected by the GPO with Headquarters Fighter Command at Stanmore. No. 11 Group covered London and the South East and included the key airfields of Hornchurch, Biggin Hill, Kenley and Tangmere.

Each of the 43 Stations had a main and an emergency operations room. Each Group possessed in addition a main and emergency filter room. The emergency rooms were replicas and were provided as far as possible with full duplication of the landline communications. They could be made available at short notice by switching arrangements at pillboxes or at a convenient telephone exchange or repeater station. Incoming enemy aircraft were detected by the long-range (60 miles – 96.5kms) CH radars. Once through the CH coastal chain, it was the responsibility of the "eyes and ears" of the volunteer Observer Corps who passed raider reports by telephone landline from Observer Posts to the Filter Rooms. These reports would specify the enemy's height, speed and course, and the number of aircraft taking part in the raid.

Other observers relayed the information in less detail to adjacent groups and to Headquarters. At the same time observers in the sector operations room passed the information obtained from the plotting table to anti-aircraft and searchlight operations rooms.

The duplications caused by reports from adjacent radar stations were spotted in the Filter Room and rationalised, so that a clear and accurate picture could be plotted on the table in Fighter Command's Operations Room. The AOC in C was thus given an overall picture of the build-up of a raid, and would be responsible for overall control of the battle.

Information stemming from the plot in Fighter Command's Operations Room was passed on to the Groups by telephone landlines; it was then relayed to the Group's sector stations, who in turn controlled their sector's fighter squadrons.

So it was that at Headquarters Fighter Command the picture on the plotting table was of the general situation obtaining throughout the whole of the fighter territory, whereas at group operations rooms a picture of the situation in its own and adjacent areas was available in greater detail. At sector stations, the situation shown in the operations room was complete down to the last detail so far as that particular area was concerned.

The Headquarters controller held a watching brief over the general progress of the battle and called in the assistance of other groups if, in his opinion, a particular group needed reinforcements. The group controller's function was to decide which sector or sectors were to deal with a raid and to instruct the controllers at those sectors as to the number of squadrons to employ. These "scramble" instructions were passed directly to the squadrons by telephone. Finally using radio-telephone communications, it was the sector controller's duty to manoeuvre his fighters into the most favourable position for interception and attack.

A vast and intricate network of GPO communications was needed to keep this complex organisation fully informed and up to date.

Bentley Priory

Penny Drew had worked at Bentley Priory as a GPO telephone operator since early 1940 when she was nineteen. The Priory was established as the Headquarters of Fighter Command in 1936. Close by is Glenthorn, Headquarters of the Anti-Aircraft Command; it was from Bentley that Air Chief Marshal Hugh Dowding fought the Battle of Britain and from Glenthorn that General Pile commanded Anti-Aircraft Command which was tasked to combat the Night Blitz of Winter 1940-41.

Penny cycled to work every morning from her parents' home in Stanmore. It was good exercise for the Priory stood on high rolling ground; from the entrance she could catch a glimpse of the spires and chimneys of north London, of Harrow Church and red-roofed suburbs.

Four hundred WAAFs worked alongside Penny and her colleagues in the Operations Room. It was unique in being the only Communications Centre in Britain which was in complete touch with all defence stations in the country. It could display tracks of aircraft over the whole of Great Britain and the sea approaches.

The principal purpose was to enable the Commander-in-Chief to see the whole "air picture" and to co-ordinate the activities of his Fighter Groups. The same information was made available for all three services – Army, Navy and Air Force.

Bentley Priory was at the heart of Air Intelligence and at the heart of Bentley Priory was the Operations Room, sited from March 1940 in an under-ground concrete bunker. Next to it, in the same bunker, was the Filter Centre, where all information was cross-checked before appearing on the map in the Operations Room, attended by WAAF plotters. This information was provided by the radar stations of Chain Home and Chain Home Low, anti-aircraft batteries and searchlight batteries and by the Royal Observer Corps, a brotherhood of remote and sometimes lonely watchers of the skies, camped out on hilltops and headlands throughout Britain. The Filter Rooms performed two functions; they identified all approaching aircraft as "hostile", "doubtful" or "friendly" and they informed Ops accordingly.

The Operations Room was the only place where aircraft tracks over the whole of Britain and the sea approaches were displayed. An exact replica is on dis-play in the RAF Museum at Hendon.

CONFIDENTIAL

HEADQUARTERS, FIGHTER COMMAND,
ROYAL AIR FORCE,
BENTLEY PRIORY,
STANMORE,
MIDDLESEX.

Telephone Nos.: BUSHEY HEATH 1681 (6 lines).
BUSHEY HEATH 1646 (4 lines).

Telegraphic Address:
"AIRGENARCH, STANMORE."

Reference :—
FC/S.19468/Sigs.

5th April, 1940.

Sir,

I have the honour to refer to the transfer
of communications from the operations and filter
rooms in Bentley Priory to the underground building
recently occupied at this Headquarters, and to draw
attention to the very valuable work carried out by
the General Post Office staff, often under very
trying circumstances, in making the necessary arrangements. The total number of operational circuits
concerned was approximately 140, and the arrangements
made by the General Post Office staff were such that,
on the occasion of the transfer, complete communication was available in the underground building
within less than one minute of the signal being given
for the transfer to take place.

2. The organisation and technical arrangements
required to produce this rapid transfer were of a
high order, and it is desired to express appreciation
of the excellent work carried out by the General Post
Office staff concerned. It is desired to draw
particular attention to the excellent services
rendered by the General Post Office Liaison Officer
at this Headquarters, Mr. E. W. Johnson, whose
efficiency and tact have been of the greatest value
in setting up and maintaining the intricate land
line communications in use in this Command.

3. I have the honour to request that an expression
of appreciation of the services above referred to may
be conveyed to the G.P.O. authorities.

I have the honour to be,
Sir,
Your obedient Servant,

H.C.T. Dowding.

Air Chief Marshal,
Air Officer Commanding-in-Chief,
Fighter Command.

The Under-Secretary of State,
Air Ministry,
Whitehall,
London, S.W.1.

1 - APR 1940

Air Chief Marshal Dowding's letter personally thanked GPO staff for their efficient transfer of communications equipment to underground HQ, Fighter Command, at Bentley Priory in 1940

81

CHAPTER SIX

Those using the room were Air Chief Marshal Hugh Dowding, Head of Fighter Command, General Pile of AA Command, the Commandant of the Observer Corps and liaison officers from Bomber and Coastal Commands, the Admiralty, the War Office and the Ministry of Home Security. It has been described by military historian John Terraine as 'the chief brain-cell of the defence of Great Britain'.

Next to the Operations Room was a Special Liaison Unit teleprinter housed in a sound-proof cubicle. The teleprinter fed the findings of ULTRA to Dowding

It was now possible for Headquarters Fighter Command to know every detail about enemy air attacks anywhere in Britain. Hurricanes and Spitfires of the RAF could be scrambled within minutes because of the pre-war telephone communication links planned and built by the GPO. In addition to the vast landline communications network provided by the GPO for raid-reporting, a complex teleprinter network was also installed and Bentley Priory became one of the centres of this network.

This 1944 photograph of London's Trafalgar Exchange's large Teleprinter Room is notable for showing the wartime all-female complement of supervisor and staff

Telephone operators in action at the GPO Exchange Headquarters, St Martins-le-Grand, London, in 1943. The switchboard is a PMB X1a, and a board listing the Emergency Services' numbers can be seen in the top right-hand corner of the photograph

The Defence Teleprinter Network (DTN)

Before the war, there had not been much demand by the Services for teleprinter communications. But early in 1938 a picture began to emerge of the possible requirements for telegraph circuits by the Admiralty and Air Ministry. The GPO Engineering Department suggested that these requirements could only be met by setting up a network, partially independent of the civil network, in which the terminal equipment should be located in Service establishments. The Services would provide accommodation for the terminal equipment and power apparatus and the GPO would be responsible for maintaining it, by keeping personnel nearby.

In 1938, the Treasury agreed that such a telegraph network would be established. It would be the same size as the existing civil network and the GPO agreed that it would be complete within three years. The scheme was dubbed "The Defence Teleprinter Network" and the name stuck.

At that time the scheme was thought to be able to provide all the telegraph requirements of the Air Ministry, the Admiralty and the War Office. The declaration of war and the course of the war meant many changes, and demand grew dramatically. The circuits provided in the network eventually extended to all parts of the British Isles and teleprinter switchboards were found in places as remote as the Orkneys and the Western Isles.

The first multi-channel voice frequency telegraph system of the DTN was opened on 31 March 1939 between Uxbridge No. 1 Repeater Station and Faraday Building in London, followed on 4 April by a system between Uxbridge No.1 and Stanmore No.1. From then on, systems opened every month until the end of the war. By the end of 1940 the provision had reached the same total as the Inland Service network itself expanding to cope with the demands of industry and government departments; by 1944 it was two and a half times bigger. Mobile terminals were also made available so that any station which might be damaged could have their service restored before a permanent replacement arrived.

The Teleprinter Network also provided for the meteorological services linking hundreds of stations scattered throughout the British Isles, and enabling each or all to be connected to a central controlling station for the simultaneous reception of information. When the Americans began to arrive in vast numbers, they created a demand for telegraph communications and again this was catered for as part of the Service requirement. GPO staff designed an adaptor which enabled American equipment to work its British counterpart and many hundreds of adaptors were provided for use by the American forces both in Britain and on the Continent. Teleprinter circuits were also set up between Britain and Washington.

By the end of the war, more than 10,000 telegraph circuits of all kinds had been provided by the GPO.

The DTN was what would be known in modern terminology as the first example of an "outsourcing contract". The DTN was still in operation, though on a much reduced scale, in 1999.

Telephone Circuits

A large number of private telephone circuits were needed by the Services for operational and administrative purposes. Before the war, only a small network of private telephone circuits had been in use. Usually they were provided by switching a number of long distance circuits from the public system at short notice to form a private network of about 500 telephone circuits (at times of coastal defence exercises etc) and a much bigger number of permanent short range circuits.

Most of the emergency circuits were switched into service at the end of August 1939 and after that most of the additional circuits needed were provided on a permanent basis. They were needed to cope with a number of changed situations. One was the added traffic following mobilisation, from the Admiralty, War Office and Air Ministry to Naval bases, Army and RAF Commands. Circuits were needed by the Observer Corps, Searchlights, AA guns and Coast Defence Artillery. They were also needed to improve communications between Commands, Stores and Depots. By August 1944, the total number of private telephone circuits in use by the Services exceeded 60,000 and the underground cabling system which had been built up during the 25 years before the war was nearly doubled during the five years of war. The 6,000,000 miles (9,655,000 km) of single wire cable had become 10,000,000 miles (16,100,000 km).

Safeguarding communications

Well before the war, provision was made by the GPO for emergency stocks of trunk cable and a number of depots were selected throughout the country where bulk reserves of a large range of sizes of cable were stored.

A large variety of special air defence and radio equipment was produced in the GPO factories which came under inspection at the London and Birmingham Test Sections. They included switchboards of various types, keyboards, transmitting and signalling equipment, plotting and controllers' tables, DTN table coders, control units, display panels, night signalling equipment and siren controls.

Clearly the ability of an organisation such as the GPO to maintain essential services both public and defence, when under attack from an enemy, is of vital importance to public security and, equally important, morale.

The objective in London was that at least one-third of the trunk and toll telephone services must be protected from disruption. Five trunk and eleven toll detached switching centres were established in London at selected exchanges alongside the main cable routes and at distances between 5-10 miles (8-16km) from the existing exchanges. They were to guard against the possible loss of the existing trunk and toll exchanges and against the severance of the cable between trunk and toll exchanges.

Steps also taken early on to cover the effects of possible damage to the Central Telegraph Office, (now the BT Centre at 81, Newgate Street, London) by the construction in underground protected accommodation of two large telegraph offices, each equipped for the immediate operation of some 100 teleprinter positions.

Every office had voice frequency telegraph equipment which could be switched to major provincial centres and could operate independently of any external source of power. One of these installations allowed telegraph traffic to continue even during air raids and when the Central Telegraph Office was destroyed by fire in December 1940, both justified their provision.

From 1941 onwards, it became established policy to decentralise the telegraph service. Further protection against enemy damage was taken by installing a large block of voice frequency telegraph terminal equipment in underground accommodation in London. Power arrangements at all the large telegraph offices were changed to ensure a 24-hour battery reserve in the case of external power supply breakdown. Finally, four mobile units were fully equipped and located at suitable points throughout the country.

In addition to the public telegraph service, the inland system was also used to provide private telegraph networks for various Ministries, the BBC, Petrol Pool and industrial organisations engaged in the war effort.

Fred Nash

Fred Nash joined the GPO in September 1935 when still too young by a year to be classified as an Unestablished Skilled Workman. After the Munich Crisis in 1938, he was almost continually engaged in providing telephone service to Army and RAF units in the Oxford area, the main one of which was the HQ of Bomber Command near High Wycombe:

"In 1942, I joined the DTN maintenance staff in the underground block at Bomber Command HQ. There were thirteen of us, some on day duty and others on night shift. I remember feeling quite overcome with the significance of the operations in which Bomber Command was involved and with the losses which occurred every day. One memorable occasion was the build up to the 1,000 bomber raid.

Some time later, I joined the crew at the underground HQ of the American 8th Army at Wycombe Abbey, the well known girls' school which had been taken over by the Americans soon after Pearl Harbour. It was interesting seeing the difference between Bomber Command ops and those of the USAAF. Bomber Command organised during the day followed by night operations while the Americans prepared at night for daytime raids. These daytime raids incurred terrific loss of life. Eventually fighter wings were set up to provide cover for the bombers and once again I was involved in setting up communications with these Wings in the Eastern counties. When the Americans went home after the war, I had to supervise the removal of all the GPO DTN equipment from the underground HQ. Later during the Cold War, the underground HQ was used again by the 8th USAAF and I became involved on a liaison basis with their Signals Section until they went home".

The War at Sea

The GPO made an immense contribution to the work of the Royal Navy and the Army, particularly in linking the ports of Plymouth, Portsmouth, Chatham, the Western Approaches and, in Scotland, Rosyth and Scapa Flow.

Cable ships were engaged from early in 1939 in laying and maintaining numerous cables for the Services and for general defence requirements. A steam lighter, the *Glencloy*, was chartered by the GPO and with a party from a cable ship, was stationed at Stromness from 1939 just to maintain and lay Service cables in the Scapa area.

Before there were sufficient naval vessels available to maintain anti-submarine cables, the GPO helped the Admiralty with this work. The submarine cables of the

various cable companies were also repaired on numerous occasions in locations rang-
ing from the South-Western Approaches to the Arctic Circle. The work was dangerous because cable ships were 'sitting targets' and a constant watch had to be kept for
the enemy. The Cable Ship *Alert* was lost with all hands on February 24, 1945 and the
Monarch was mined on April 16 that same year (see page 97).

The Battle of the Atlantic

Germany intended to starve Britain into surrender by destroying the ships
which brought food and other vital supplies into the country. It was said that the Battle
of the Atlantic was a fight to secure the life-line of Great Britain. Attacks on shipping
were made from the air, by U-boats and by surface ships. To counter these threats, ships
were formed into convoys with as much air and surface protection as possible. The
Headquarters of the Convoy organisation was initially at Plymouth but after the fall
of France, when the whole of the
south coast was vulnerable to air
attack, the organisation moved to
Liverpool.

GPO Engineers repair damaged trunking in the Liverpool Telephone Exchange Cable Chamber after an enemy bombing raid on 3-4 August 1941

Derby House, Liverpool, was
the Headquarters of Western Approaches Command, from where the
Battle of the Atlantic was fought and
won. The organisation was in every
sense a combined one requiring the
joint administration of the Navy and
RAF. The naval organisation comprised the Officers in charge of the
ports of Cardiff, Milford Haven,
Bristol, Greenock, Glasgow,
Londonderry and Belfast. The RAF
organisation known as No.15 Group
was a Group of Coastal Command
created to fight in the Atlantic battle.
The bases were sited as near the scene
of operations as possible. The huge
network of communications established by the GPO became the nervous system of the organisation which
controlled this tremendous battle.

The new headquarters was a

concrete fortress with a 7ft 6in(2.3m) roof and 3ft 6in(1.0m) wall constructed in the basement and lower ground floors to house operational staff and their communications plant. The work was completed in January 1941 with staff working round the clock in spite of almost nightly air raids. A reserve headquarters was equipped at Knowsley Hall, eleven miles from Liverpool. All equipment was duplicated and over 150 circuits could be switched at seven different points. Fortunately it was never required in actual service.

An idea of the huge amount of operational and administrative traffic generated at Liverpool can be gained from the fact that naval personnel under the Commander-in-Chief's Command numbered over 100,000.

On an average day 700/800 signals were handled in the Naval Signal Office which was equipped with 20 teleprinters; the number of signals sometimes soared to 1,400. The RAF Signals Section had over 50 teleprinters working on operational and administrative circuits.

Up to date weather information was vital both to those at sea and in the air. Incorporated in the Group was an Air Ministry meteorological broadcast unit which collected weather observations from all parts of Britain. In addition a transatlantic meteorological bulletin was continually received by teleprinter from the "Transat" headquarters.

Ron Pidgley

"I was with the GPO from 1937-1980 and during the war was a Royal Signals Instrument mechanic. In 1941 I volunteered for Special Service duties, and Christmas that year found me maintaining the No. 18 radio sets of the Commando Regimental Signals and the Royal Signal control set No. 11 on the bridge of HMS Kenya. We were part of the flotilla which was to mount a commando raid on the enemy in Norway.

The weather was very bad and before proceeding the flotilla anchored at Sullum Voe in the Shetlands for 24 hours. We entered the narrow Fjord just before dawn and took the enemy by surprise, still sleeping off their Christmas celebrations. The Commando landed, took prisoners, set fire to the fish oil factories and took on board a number of Quislings and Norwegians anxious to serve with the Allies. Our ship was continually targeted from the shore while this was going on, but the operation was successful; it was the first real penetration into the German stronghold in Europe".

Remote control wireless telegraph circuits were set up from Liverpool to stations scattered over the British Isles. These circuits were all duplicated on alternative routes because of their importance. In all over 420 private circuits radiated from Allied Central Headquarters (ACHQ), many of them several hundred miles long.

The equipment in Derby House included an automatic house telephone system and loud-speaking equipment enabling the Commander-in-Chief and his staff to confer without the assistance of an operator and to facilitate the daily joint conference with the Admiralty, Coastal Command and other Commanders-in-Chief.

On the huge war plot in the Operations Room, submarine symbols represented the U-boats and each convoy route was shown by a different coloured elastic tape. The communications by GPO landline telephone and teleprinters between Western Approaches and the Admiralty were so effective that no formal War Diary was kept at Derby House, nor were the usual monthly command reports sent to the Admiralty.

During the first week of May 1941, there was an all out eight-night blitz on the centre of Liverpool. The building containing the three main GPO Exchanges was burnt out and ACHQ lost virtually all of its communications. By dint of extraordinary efforts, however, the restoration of most circuits was completed within ten days. It was just in time. On 22 May the *Bismarck* and her escorts left Norway to destroy Britain's shipping – the timing was almost certainly deliberate following the blitz on Liverpool. But ACHQ had survived the blitz and was able to co-ordinate and control the search which ended so successfully with the sinking of the *Bismarck* on 27 May. It was just one example of the way in which the

Members of a German artillery unit shown encoding messages on an Enigma machine. Success in breaking this code at Bletchley Park by Alan Turing and others played a major part in the Allied victory. The officer is General Heinz Guderian, General of Panzer troops

Bletchley Park, top secret wartime centre where the German ENIGMA and other codes were broken, and the forerunner of modern computers was invented

GPO helped Britain to fight and eventually to win the Battle of the Atlantic.

ENIGMA and ULTRA

The ENIGMA machine, developed by the German inventor Dr. Arthur Schervius in the 1920s, was intended to prevent industrial espionage by encoding correspondence. The German Navy adopted it in 1926 to encode military messages and the German Army followed suit in 1928.

During World War Two the German Army, Navy and Air Force used the ENIGMA Machine, which looked like an over-grown typewriter, to encode their signals believing it provided an unbreakable system. It could provide almost limitless combinations, all instantly changeable by resetting the rotor wheels and electrical connections. The German High Command thought that the ENIGMA Code was unbreakable but Polish Intelligence succeeded in acquiring one of the ENIGMA machines. By July 1939 they had begun to unpick the machine's cipher system and invited French and British cryptographers to a secret meeting in the Pyre Forest in Poland in July 1939 to share their findings with them. When war broke out just two months later, the Poles made sure that a model of the ENIGMA machine found its way back via the RAF to

Dr Thomas 'Tommy' Flowers, inventor of the COLOSSUS computer in 1943. He won The Martlesham Medal in 1980 for his work on electronic switching

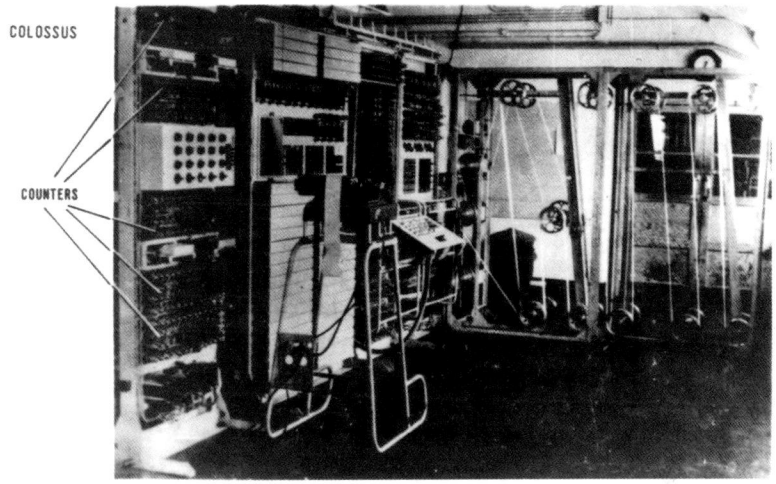

COLOSSUS

COUNTERS

The first major computer created at Bletchley Park in 1943, huge by modern standards, was appropriately named COLOSSUS. The Mark 1 version was powered by 1,500 valves, the Mark 2 by no less than 2,500

Bletchley Park, the Government's Code and Cypher School (GCCS) which controlled all British cryptanalysis.

Here the brightest and best of Britain's young scientists were recruited after the outbreak of war. Their first priority was to break the ENIGMA Codes. This was a monumental and enormously time-consuming task. As the workload at Bletchley increased, it became clear that automation was vital in order to process the volume of traffic.

The engineers from the GPO Research Station at Dollis Hill were invited to help with machines which would do this. First came the refined 'bombes' – electro-mechanical machines about 6ft high and about 6 ft wide (1.8m x 1.8m). In their earliest form they had been devised by the Polish codebreakers. The bombes proved to be the mechanical bridge between manual codebreaking and the computer age which began with COLOSSUS in late 1943. The bombes were housed at Bletchley in 'Hut 11a' which was not a hut at all but a massively constructed concrete structure with walls 2 feet (0.6m) thick and a roof of interlocking concrete slabs cemented together with a concrete covering over the top. The roof was supported by 15 inch (367mm) steel girders embedded in the concrete floor and the walls contained more steel girders at 2 ft (0.6m) intervals. It was in this building that the first ENIGMA codes were broken mechanically from 1 August 1940 onwards. After Churchill became Prime Minister, he referred to Bletchley as his 'secret' and, from 1941, the secret intelligence gathered and relayed by the Park's codebreakers was code-named ULTRA; it was the greatest secret of the war. It had to be carefully used to ensure that the Germans did not realise that their codes had been broken.

Work continued throughout the war into improving the speed with which coded signals could be handled. To Sir Herbert Leon's apple, pear and plum store at Bletchley Park, by now converted into what became known as 'The Bungalow', came Alan Turing, who worked on his own for days at a time on what we now know to be computer research. He was joined by Dr Tommy Flowers from Dollis Hill. Between them they devised what they called the 'Heath Robinson' machine, a mass of cogs, valves and pulleys supplementing the advanced electronics which they hoped would break the high grade German codes more quickly.

The machine worked and became the forerunner of the world's first electronic programmable computer, 'COLOSSUS' which was assembled in the Park in December 1943 and played a full part in codebreaking activity by the time of the D-Day landings in June 1944.

Allied troops photographed landing on the Normandy beaches on D-Day, 6 June 1944. Signallers were operating alongside the combat troops to provide vital communications links as the drive to liberate Europe gathered speed

Peter Archer's painting 'Swiftly Ashore' shows 3ʳᵈ Infantry Divisional Signal Regiment regrouping at la Breche d'Hermanville after landing on D-Day. The work was commissioned by 3ʳᵈ (UK) Division HQ and Signal Regiment, and painted in 1995

COLOSSUS was a formidable piece of equipment. It stood some 16 ft long, 8 ft high and about 12 feet deep (4.9 x 2.4 x 3.7m) in places and gave Bletchley Park the honour of being the birthplace of the computer-led society in which we now live. This was kept a secret for 30 years and only became known in 1975.

By 1944, the Ultra Team had 6,000 experts waiting to decrypt and decode raw intelligence.

Overseas Activity

Outside Britain, civilian telephone systems were used where possible, augmented by military circuits and instruments. The field telephones available, the D Mark 5 and the Telephone F, did not provide satisfactory speech over more than ten miles. These sets were made more sensitive and new sets were introduced including the Apparatus Carrying Telephone, 1+1, with a range of 40 to 50 miles and the Telephone-F, a high-power telephone, which operated like a radio-telephone. New style telephones, the L and J were produced and Field Exchanges were also developed which were more robust and versatile than those available in 1939.

During the War over 1mn telephones, 4mn miles of field cable and some 8,000 Field Exchanges were produced by British industry. The telephone, although less versatile than wireless, played a major role in the Army's communication in all theatres.

Planning for the Normandy Invasion

As D-Day approached, demands for new telecommunications equipment reached their peak. A huge construction programme was begun, to facilitate the control of the Normandy Invasion. Hundreds of miles of cable were laid, switchboards, telephones and teleprinters were installed along the south coast of England. At Bentley Priory, a large new switchboard had been installed. After D-Day it handled calls between Home and Allied Forces in North-West Europe. By VE Day there was direct communication with Brussels, Stuttgart, Hamburg and eventually Berlin.

In 1944, George Single was still in Dover. In the years which had passed since Dunkirk, he had been busy working on one of the most intriguing telecommunication constructions of the war – a huge Intercommunications Centre deep inside the cliff-face, only a few steps from Naafi's famous Calais View Canteen. The spectacular view over the harbour never failed to dazzle him nor, on clear days, the silhouette of Calais and the low sand dunes between Calais and Boulogne:

"Behind a camouflaged opening in the cliff face there was a series of winding passages and underground galleries, miles of cable and vast quantities of telephone, teleprinter and radar equipment. Work had begun six years earlier during the Munich crisis when the War Office foresaw the need for a complete system of intercommunication between Whitehall and the South Coast ports. Those years behind the cliff-face were among the most memorable of my life.

By 1944 a complete Communications Centre had been built. It was big enough to serve as the General Headquarters of an entire Expeditionary Force. There were three large adjoining Operations Rooms for each of the three services and this enabled Combined Operations to take place".

When this secret citadel was completed, it could have served as GHQ for the British Liberation Army on D-Day had the invasion been launched from Kent, as the Germans were led to believe.

Plans for the liberation of Europe after D-Day

After Dunkirk, all the cross-Channel cable connections to the Continent which had been built up since before World War One were cut.

The Wireless Set No 10, shown here in a contemporary photograph, became something of an icon in the history of military communications because of its long life and rugged reliability

Peter Archer's painting of Corporal Thomas Waters, MM who laid and maintained a telephone communications link single-handed under fire during the fierce battle for the Caen Canal Bridge

From that date on, it was realised that the rebuilding of the large network which had existed would be necessary at some future date to support an army on the Continent and this was kept under constant review.

All planning and preparations for D-Day had to be carried out in total secrecy. For the South Coast Submarine Cable Scheme, the title given to the provision of cable communications for the liberating forces, there was little advance information available. But, unlike peacetime, when it could all be done at a leisurely pace, communication circuits would be required as soon as a cable had been landed.

Discussions between the GPO and the military began in 1942 and in 1943 a number of strategic landing points were chosen in the south of England. At some of these, special blast-protected, partially underground buildings were erected. They were built to accommodate the estimated amount of terminal equipment and submarine cable which might be needed from each landing point. Where possible the buildings were positioned near the main cable routes to facilitate the extension of circuits in Britain, and to avoid the danger of German Commando raids they were sited a short distance inland.

The distance between the strategic landing points in the south of England and those on the continent varied between 20 and 125 nautical miles (32 – 200 km), and it was decided to use standard concentric type submarine cable throughout. Three types of carrier terminal equipment were used. The first provided three speech and six voice frequency telegraph channels over any length of submarine cable up to 125 nautical miles. The second could provide twelve speech circuits and one speaker circuit on any cable length up to 65 nautical miles. For this type of equipment it was necessary to specify the areas in France which could be used as landing points for cable to carry twelve circuits.

The third type of equipment could provide 60 channels on one cable but could only be used on cable lengths of up to 30 nautical miles. This ruled out all channel routes other than the Straits of Dover. Two complete sets of this type of equipment were designed and built at the GPO Research Station. That for the British side was installed in the repeater station of Dover Combined Headquarters and linked to the landing points at Abbottscliffe and St Margaret's Bay.

Once landed on the Continent it was envisaged that mobile equipment would be connected to the cable in the first instance so that almost immediate service could be provided. This would be followed later by erecting a transportable set of equipment, so releasing the mobile equipment for use around the coast as the operation proceeded.

Loading of the cable ships began in December 1943 and was completed in May 1944. Large scale mining operations in the seaways and attacks on shipping by air and sea had been expected and arrangements had therefore been made for the voyages of the cable ships to be reduced to a minimum. A merchant ship was used as a cable store. Based at a convenient point, the cable ships could berth alongside at short notice to load whatever stocks they needed.

The first cable was laid by the two GPO ships *Iris* and *Alert*. The landing point in England was at Southbourne near Bournemouth and the *Iris* started laying the cable on Thursday 8 June. The *Alert* landed the cable at Longues on the Normandy beachhead at midnight on the following day. The first telephone conversation from Europe to Britain since 1940 immediately took place and by the night of 12 June three speech and six telegraph channels were available. From those first channel links thousands and thousands of miles of telephone and telegraph cables were laid following the advancing armies through North- West Europe. Wherever possible they made use of surviving civilian networks.

The Cable Ships

During World War Two, the GPO had four Telegraph Ships – the Ariel, Iris, *Monarch* and *Alert*. Cable Officer Simon Jameson served on the *Monarch* for the period leading up to D-Day and beyond. Based in the cable depot at Dover, his task immediately following D-Day in June 1944 was to lay and maintain GPO cables between England and France following the arrival of waves of British and American troops:

"By that stage in the war, multiple-core cables were being used. This

HMTS Monarch *was one of the Royal Navy's Telegraph Ships, sunk by enemy action in 1944*

enabled a number of messages to be sent at the same time. The cable itself was stored in great coils in three circular tanks in the middle of the ship. My job was to make sure that the cable remained in tiptop condition and to supervise the cable laying operation. The cable was hauled out by a powerful engine on the forward deck and paid out over a sheave set in the bow.

From the Chart Room behind the Captain's bridge, I could see the Straits of Dover criss-crossed with lines like a gridiron. The cables which ran across were ocean cables. They linked German North Sea ports with America and the West Indies These cables were cut and out of action for the whole of the war. The cross-lines were British GPO cables which ran from England to France. They kept the Force commanders in direct touch with Headquarters at home."

In 1944, the *Monarch* was sunk. Those who perished were commemorated by the launch in 1945 of a new *Monarch*. She became the largest cable ship afloat with a gross tonnage of 8,200 tons.

In Britain itself, an inland network of high grade telephone circuits was built up during the twelve months before D-Day for the British and American military, naval and air forces. They connected the main and subsidiary Combined Headquarters and other Service establishments with the submarine cable repeater stations and the twelve

Army cross-Channel radio-telephone stations which were scattered along the South Coast between Dover and Plymouth.

Bomber Command

As Britain went over to the offensive, the GPO faced new challenges. By mid 1944, Headquarters Bomber Command had five Operational Groups with five stations in each group, and there were three squadrons in each station. Elsewhere there were 24 RAF stations engaged in operational training.

The growth of the landline network kept pace with the increase in the bomber force and the extent of the expansion is indicated by the following figures:

	1939	1945
PBX positions	32	472
Telephone stations	1,250	15,200
Teleprinters	20	640
Private Wires, Speech	40	875
Private Wires, Teleprinter	20	985

David Buckley, York *(GPO 1943-1960)*

Just a bit too prompt!

"I joined the GPO Engineering Department as a "Youth in Training" in February 1943. About eighteen months later I was sent to HQ 4 Group Bomber Command at Heslington Hall (now York University) to help maintain what was known as the "Defence Telecommunications Network". It consisted of a network of voice and telegraph channels, which were routed over a series of voice frequency (VF) systems.

One of the links was the Meteorological channel which collected weather reports every hour and broadcast them for the next 50 minutes. Any faults on this channel had to be corrected pronto. On one occasion we were a little too prompt! A fault was reported at RAF Pocklington, a squadron headquarters. Our engineer was dispatched and in his enthusiasm to deal with the fault took a short cut round the perimeter track to the Met office in the control tower at the far side of the airfield. He did not realise that the squadron were assembling for take off as part of a bombing raid and as his little green van, going like a bat out of hell, met them coming in the opposite direction, his surprise must have been as great as theirs!

The squadron's timing was so disrupted that they could not take part in the raid and the outcome was a severe reprimand. Nobody dared to venture onto the perimeter track of any base after that!"

Because of the division of responsibility between the air and administration staffs and to ensure that there was no delay in the transmission of operational messages, two separate communication networks were provided, Operations and Administration, to all formations.

The importance of the landline system which served Bomber Command was recognised in a letter sent to the Postmaster-General by Air Chief Marshal Sir Arthur Harris, Commander-in-Chief, on 22 May 1945. He wrote:

> *"In this hour of achievement of victory in Europe, I wish to express my appreciation of the invaluable work performed by the GPO in providing and maintaining the land line communication system used by Bomber Command.*
>
> *The first requirement of the bomber offensive is efficient communication. The ability to carry out detailed planning without delay and to co-ordinate the bombing effort in the light of the most recent Intelligence information is of the utmost importance. Rapid transmission of information to headquarters and of operational orders to squadrons is, therefore, essential, and can only be obtained from a highly developed and flexible communication system.*
>
> *This the GPO has provided in Bomber Command throughout the war. Not only has the land line network met the operational requirement referred to above, but it has also been a prime factor in reducing the difficulties of administration which are inevitable in such a highly centralised and complex organisation as Bomber Command. Furthermore landlines have played an essential part in the use of many offensive and defensive devices and have thus been instrumental in the saving of bomber aircraft and their crews."*

The Avro Lancaster 1 of No 514 Squadron RAF in 1944. The heavy bombing raids carried out by Lancasters played a major part in bringing the war in Europe to an end

1945-1980: THE COLD WAR

By the time Germany surrendered in 1945, the country was in ruins. Frequent heavy bombing raids had reduced much of Berlin and other major cities to heaps of rubble. The capital, divided into Allied zones, became the starting point of the Cold War between East and West

Introduction

The end of World War Two did not bring the hoped-for peace. Germany was in ruins, Italy in chaos. Japan had been devastated by the two atomic bombs. The former Allies set about rebuilding their own shattered countries with very different aims. Until galvanised into providing what became known as Marshall Aid, America felt that the occupied countries and their European allies should help themselves. Russia saw the shattered countries of Europe as an opportunity to establish world communism, and soon held Hungary, Poland, Romania, Bulgaria and Czechoslovakia in an iron grip.

In February 1946 Joseph Stalin, in his first big speech since the end of the Second World War, allocated the Soviet defence industries the major part of the

NATIONAL SERVICE

The postwar shortage of money inevitably conditioned and constrained UK defence policy, making the large numbers of wartime armed forces impossibly expensive to maintain. Demobilisation proceeded apace, to be followed by further cuts, and faced by increasing worldwide commitments the manpower shortfall was balanced by the introduction of National Service.

Bill Findlay, a former GPO man now living in Glasgow, remembers that the re-introduction of National Service in 1945 provided an important link between Military Communications and the GPO. All fit young men were obliged to serve with the armed forces for eighteen months and were called up just before their nineteenth birthday. They were exempted only to complete their apprenticeship or degree studies.

"In those days, GPO engineering 'apprentices' served a two-year course to qualify as a Technician, then trained for another two years to become a Technical Officer. Under an agreement reached between the GPO and the War Office, the young apprentices were called up on completion of their first two-year course and were then directed towards a suitable technical unit where they could spend the next two years.

Some GPO men joined the Royal Air Force, some the Royal Navy and a handful served in other Army regiments, but the vast majority found themselves in the Royal Signals, at that time based in Catterick. Every two weeks, hundreds of young men could be seen at Darlington Railway Station waiting to catch the "Catterick Flier", and a little later they would be welcomed by NCOs from 7 Training Regiment, Royal Signals.

After four weeks Induction Training – also known as Square Bashing – the young soldiers were allocated a trade and most of them were destined to become Radio, Line or Teleprinter Technicians, involving an intensive 22-week training course in Catterick. Around 90 per cent of these young men had served their apprenticeship with the GPO and most returned to the GPO when their two years were up. When they had finished their training, most were assigned to field posts and often took on responsible jobs either in Royal Signal units or with other regiments. Some remained as Instructors at Catterick and became NCOs. A very few applied for commissions".

Many of those who did not stay at Catterick saw service in Europe, the Middle East and the Far East and some were involved in active service. Almost all were given the chance of working on advanced technological equipment and this helped them in their GPO careers, along with the discipline of teamwork on which army life depends.

national budget in an effort to modernise Russia's military forces to something approaching technical parity with the West. A month later Winston Churchill made his famous "Iron Curtain" speech at Fulton, Missouri, and thus began what was to become known as the "Cold War".

Before long, Europe was divided into two armed camps by the Iron Curtain. The Soviet Bloc and the Western Allies carried out a propaganda and espionage war which lasted until 1990. The Cold War threatened to escalate into another World War in 1948 during the Berlin Airlift, and again in 1962 during the Cuban Missile Crisis.

The Re-shaping of Britain's Air Defences

The end of the European War in May 1945 saw the RAF at its largest in terms of aircraft and manpower in the whole of its short history; 9,200 first line aircraft and a manpower strength of 1,079,835, of which 193,313 were aircrew. Its post-war size was dictated by several factors, chief amongst which was the need to drastically reduce the Defence Budget in as short a time as possible to fend off national bankruptcy. Second was the need to return as many servicemen (and women) as possible to civilian life and third, to assess the impact of new technology (jet engines, radar and related electronic devices and the atomic bomb) on the size and form of the RAF. All of which needed to be considered if the RAF was to continue as a modern and viable fighting force.

By the end of the Second World War, a very extensive radar-reporting chain existed which covered the whole country. It was supported by a vast telecommunications network of speech circuits and telegraph lines which had been installed by the GPO.

In 1946 Group Captain John Cherry, a staff officer at Headquarters Fighter Command, was appointed to carry out a thorough investigation of the UK network. The objective was to propose a system capable of intercepting and destroying Russian nuclear bombers at long range. It was to be several years, however, before the Cherry Report, published in the mid-1950s, concluded that the entire air defence organisation needed restructuring and modernising.

The Defence White Paper of 1947 foresaw a post-war world dominated by atomic weapons and proposed a period of "transition" during which the country might draw breath. National Service was to be retained throughout this period and the White Paper highlighted the need to preserve the integrity and continuity of the RAF. The Government considered that war was unlikely within five years, but might occur in the second five. This assessment was based on intelligence reports of the Soviet Forces' capability and the assurance that Britain might shelter under the nuclear umbrella of the United States. Whatever the reason, by June 1948 the RAF's strength was reduced to 25 squadrons in Fighter Command, 24 in Bomber Command, 20 in Transport Command and 11 in Coastal Command. Regular manpower was also seriously curtailed; 375,000 in 1948, falling to 325,000 in 1949. However, the Royal Auxiliary Air Force was re-established in 1947 to provide a ready supply of experienced ex-RAF air and ground crews to bolster the regulars in times of tension. Many of these squadrons were allocated to Fighter Command.

The air defence system that had been built up gradually during the War provided one of the best, if not the best, systems of its type anywhere in the world. However, in the immediate post-war period Great Britain, the United States and Russia were all developing inter-continental atomic bombers, whose speed and range rendered the UK's fighter and radar defences obsolescent. Instead of having to detect, track and intercept relatively slow moving bombers, Fighter Command would have to contend with fast, high flying jet bombers and control their equally fast intercepting jet fighters. Nevertheless, the principal objectives of the air defence network remained the same; to detect and intercept the enemy as far away from the shores of Great Britain as was possible. This implied the need to control greater amounts of airspace

The Type 80 radar, introduced in 1954. This considerably advanced design enabled the RAF's air defence system to meet the threat of supersonic aircraft. Operating on 3000 m/hz (10 cm wavelength), it had a range of well over 200 miles

Type 64 Radar console with a Post Office keyboard

from fewer, but higher powered radar stations.

The old air defence sectors were abolished and in their place six new ones were instituted, controlling greater amounts of airspace. Still covering the whole of the UK, the new sectors were allocated a sector controller who had the authority to "scramble" fighters within his sector. To complete the interception, control was passed to Ground Control Interception (GCI) stations within the local area for close control of the attack.

The types of aircraft in Fighter Command had also changed. By 1951 most of the wartime piston-engined fighters, the Spitfire, Tempest and Typhoon and the night-fighting Mosquito had gone, to be replaced by jet-engined fighters of much greater performance. The two principal fighters of the period were the Vampire and Meteor in both the single-seat day-fighter role and the two-seat night-fighter role.

The GPO was kept very busy during this period. Those radar stations declared surplus to require-

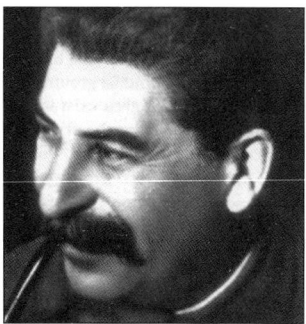

Joseph Stalin, 1879-1953, leader of the Russian people for nearly 30 years, saw the devastation in Europe as a chance to bring more states under Communist rule with a view to eventual world domination

ments were removed from the network, but fortunately their equipment and cable were not recovered immediately. Speech and telegraph circuits were disconnected from the national transmission network and allocated to civilian telecommunications. Engineers were stood down from defence work to satisfy the growing demand for telephone service. Like everyone else the GPO was returning to "normal" life!

The beginning of the Early Warning System

In 1949 the USSR conducted their first atom bomb tests. In response, the US upgraded their radar capability to counter the increased speed of aircraft and their frequent change of position. Early warning stations – the DEW Line – were constructed across the whole of North America; they could detect any plane approaching on a polar route. But even the DEW line could not supply information fast enough for the intercontinental missile threat. A new system was therefore developed with three powerful radar installations in England, Alaska and Greenland, able to detect missiles at 3,000 miles. And so the legendary fifteen-minute warning was born.

A Chiefs of Staff paper in March 1949 concluded that the UK was virtually defenceless if no warning of an attack could be given. The British government's White Paper underlined the need for new equipment, including telecommunications and radar systems. Only a month later, the North Atlantic Treaty was signed, creating the cornerstone of future British defence policy and security. In December 1949, NATO called for the defences of the free world to be strengthened. Next year, a new UK defence programme was announced. Reservists were called up for regular training; defence production expenditure was to be quadrupled by 1953.

Two years would be required before proper radar cover could be provided. The radars were in need of improvement. A number of major defence companies were called in to help. In June 1950 the UK part of this plan was given the code-name ROTOR. Under this plan, the sixteen year old Type 7 Chain Home (CH) radars at the most important Ground Control Interception (GCI) sites were recovered and replaced by Type 80 sets which gave a much improved coverage – ranges up to 200 nautical miles (354 kms) and heights up to 40,000 ft (12,200m).

To provide some degree of protection for the radars and their operating personnel, the Sector Operation Centres (SOC) and GCI stations were moved into underground shelters. Fortunately most of the wartime CH and GCI sites had not been abandoned and it proved possible to re-use some of the buildings and most of the telephone cabling. The ROTOR programme within the GPO involved the supporting telecommunications network being reconfigured and substantially increased cabling with some new private circuits and teleprinter lines to be provided at those sites designated as SOCs.

Even ROTOR radars fell short of what was needed, but no new designs were as yet forthcoming and both the Naval Type 984 set and the Army set ORANGE YEOMAN were considered as alternatives.

In March 1953 Joseph Stalin died, and an armistice brought the Korean War to an end. A state of Cold War now existed and, once again, the urgency went out of the need for improved UK air defences.

This did not last long. Everything changed when the Russians exploded their first atomic bomb in August 1953. It was clear that the UK urgently needed a new air defence policy, but what? The concept of defence by deterrence was emerging only gradually. In 1954 the Air Defence Committee decided that close defence of vulnerable points would be useless. The main aim must be to destroy the high-speed, high-altitude nuclear bomber before it reached the UK coast.

The Cherry Report, published in the mid-1950s, proposed a more powerful radar network with the main area of active defence focused on the East Coast of England and Scotland, and around London. Meanwhile, work continued on the ROTOR system which was handed over to Fighter Command in April 1956. ROTOR provided Fighter Command with full Control and Reporting cover along the whole of the East and South-east coasts, and limited cover over the remainder of the UK.

However, the design of the system still maintained the World War Two pattern in which the reporting or early warning role, and the GCI role, were completely separate, inevitably causing delays and errors.

However, ROTOR did provide an interim solution to the air defence problem. It included support for the V-bombers, the Vulcans, Victors and Valiants, which were on quick reaction duty along the East Coast.

The problems of Control and Reporting (C&R) remained, and Fighter Command's new proposal, scheduled for implementation by 1958, was for an integrated C&R system which would take over many responsibilities from the old sector operation centres. Considerable savings would be possible both in manpower and equipment. The scheme was accepted by the Air Council on 21 June 1956 but very little had been achieved by the time that the Cold War nuclear threat was addressed in the Defence White Papers of 1956 and 1957. The 1957 document spelt out the details, laying down the basic fact that 'Atomic weapons and rocket weapons, offensive and defensive, must alter the whole basis of military planning'. The new defence aims were to act jointly with other NATO allies, and to defend British colonies and protected territories.

The UK deterrent would include nuclear missiles, V-bombers and fighters, and in due course the aircraft would be supplemented by a ground-to-air guided missile system. Cost was, as always, a determining factor. With the new NATO-born strategy of collective security, however, defence was no longer the concern of individual countries. As far back as 1953, NATO military headquarters at SHAPE had first begun to consider an integrated air defence system. This requirement was formalised in August 1961 and represented the sum of all the individual proposals by NATO countries. The basis of the system was formed by the UK Plan Ahead system, which had been re-christened LINESMAN.

The system became known as the NATO Air Defence Ground Environment, or NADGE. It was given the go-ahead in March 1962.

By the early 1970s, much of the NADGE equipment had been installed. At the same time the Alliance had re-assessed the threat from the Warsaw Pact and was no longer committed to defence by massive nuclear retaliation; the concept of flexible response had become NATO policy. This ensured the future of LINESMAN, and proposals were made to augment and ultimately transform it into what became the United Kingdom Air Defence Ground Environment – UKADGE – part of the NATO Air Defence System.

The implementation of the LINESMAN system depended a great deal on communications for its day-to-day operation. Unlike the ROTOR system, LINESMAN relied on a network of private automatic branch exchanges (PABX) to reduce the number of point-to-point private circuits hitherto employed for communication between fighter airfields, radar stations and SOCs. Calls were routed by a switched network, however, in order to avoid the users having to remember literally hundreds of telephone numbers, the system was designed around automatic "programmable★" keysenders. Controllers, and alike, would therefore select the circuit they required on a keyboard (something akin to a key and lamp unit) and the keysender would automatically "dial" the correct digits to route that call to its destination.

To avoid too complex a network and to provide an interface to the civil air traffic control network run by the National Air Traffic Control Service, many of the calls were routed through the London Air Traffic Control Centre at West Drayton on the western outskirts of London.

Co-ordination of the design of the keysender equipment and the provision of the hundreds of high quality inter-PABX circuits, some of which employed voice frequency signalling for the first time, was the responsibility of the GPO's Telecommunications Headquarters. They had the job of providing all the inter-PABX circuits. Their Air Defence Group (usually referred to by the RAF and the GPO as the

★ See footnote at end of chapter

A DIGNIFIED EXIT: A J Mashford

"For nearly four years from September 1962, I was responsible for the provision of telephone service to the Royal Family and the Government. My job was to decide how each need should be met and to issue the appropriate instructions. It was a 24-hour, 365-day a year job.

When the first NATO Ministerial Conference was held at Lancaster House in London in May 1965, government instructions were quite clear. The standard had to be set for all future NATO Conferences and the reputation of the British Telecommunications industry jealously maintained. As part of the brief, a telephone service in the NATO Secretary-General's office was to be available day and night for the duration. There I was on the day the conference was due to open, relaxing in the grounds of Lancaster House, checking through everything in my mind, wondering if the last 'i' had been dotted and the last 't' crossed. It was then that Lord Hood from the Foreign Office dashed up to me. The Secretary-General's phone was not working. All the telephone engineers had left the site. I had not had 'hands on' experience for many years.

With the aid of a nail file, I removed various covers from the equipment fitted within the knee-hole of the Secretary-General's desk and diagnosed 'mains failure'. Until that point, I did not know that within Lancaster House, the telephone socket outlets were on the same circuit as the lights! Furthermore, there were no light switches within that room. If a light had to be switched on or off, the Butler had to be summoned and the request made to him. In a nutshell, the phone would only work if the chandelier above the desk was on. I gave the Butler clear instructions that under no circumstances was the chandelier light to be switched off, day or night, for the duration of the conference.

Having restored the telephone to working order, I began to replace the various covers. On emerging from the desk, I was dismayed to see to my right, between me and the door, two lines of people. They were the Senior Members of our Government and Armed Forces. The Secretary-General was being introduced to those in the front row! There was no escape! I joined the end of the second row, shook hands with the Secretary-General and when the party moved to refreshments at the far end of the room, made my exit".

AD Group), headed by Mr Fleetwood, was given the responsibility for the design, installation and maintenance of the keysenders and keyboards. The task of designing the keysenders was given to Les Saunders, who produced a unit that relied on transistors to undertake much of the memory and marking logic. Indeed it is thought that the LINESMAN keysender was the first operational use of germanium transistors in the GPO.

Development of the system was begun in 1964 and such was its complexity, it was not completed until 1967. The manufacture of the large numbers of keysenders was beyond the capacity of the AD Group's wiring contractors and the work was entrusted to L. M. Ericsson at Nottingham for the quantity production. The keyboards and other smaller amounts of equipment were however built by the AD Group's own contractors.

Each radar station, fighter airfield, SOC and fighter headquarters was provided with a PABX (electro-mechanical in those days), through and from which the LINESMAN calls originated, or were routed. The project management of all of these nodes was broken down into the various component areas and given an engineer to oversee the implementation. Thus, airfields were the responsibility of Wally Setchfield, radar stations and SOCs came under Alf Woolar and Tom Behan and HQ Fighter Command was the responsibility of Charles Bignell and John Baxter. The, what we would now refer to as "systems engineering" or "systems integration," of all these sites fell to George Young.

Work began on providing the PABXs, the keysenders and keyboards and inter-PABX circuits in 1967 and was duly completed ready for service by 1969. Later on another system modelled on LINESMAN was built for the NATS (National Air Traffic Service) by George Young, John Baxter and John O'Connor and completed in the mid-seventies.

The LINESMAN network represented one of the most complex tasks undertaken by the GPO, outside of the provision of the public telephone network.

The V-Bomber Force

The UK detonated their first nuclear weapon, a plutonium A-bomb, off North-Western Australia on 3 October 1952, and became the third nation to join the A-Bomb Club after the United States and the Soviet Union. The bombs weighed 10,000lb (4,536kg) and they could not be carried to their targets in the Soviet Union in the RAF's standard piston engined bomber, the Avro Lincoln. During 1946, the RAF issued a specification for a four-engined jet propelled bomber capable of carrying the weapon over 3,350 miles (5,391km), at speeds up to 500kts (885km/hr), at an altitude of 45,000ft (13,716m). The aircraft would carry a crew of five – two pilots, two navigator/bomb-aimers and an electronics countermeasurers operator – but no defensive armament.

Four companies bid for the project, which was won jointly by Avro with the Vulcan and Handley Page with their Victor. Vickers was awarded a stop-gap contract to supply Valiants as an insurance against the failure of the more sophisticated designs. It was from these V-named aircraft that Bomber Command's V-Force got their title. The Valiant was the first to enter service early in 1955. The Vulcan B1 followed during February 1957, then the Victor B1 in November of the same year.

By 1962 the V-Force had reached their zenith when three squadrons of Valiants for in-flight refuelling, nine of Vulcans and six of Victors were deployed at seven UK stations – Marham, Waddington, Cottesmore, Honington, Scampton, Wittering and Coningsby.

The vulnerability of these airfields to a pre-emptive Soviet strike while the aircraft were still on the ground concerned the Government and the RAF. The United States Air Force overcame the problem by having a proportion of their B-52 bombers airborne at all times. The V-bombers did not lend themselves to this approach. The practical solution was to hold a proportion of the Force on high ground alert, and so Quick Reaction Alert (QRA) was born. With constant alert exercises, this then became an all-pervasive feature of life in the V-Force.

Every V-Force station provided accommodation for up to three bomber squadrons. Aircraft on Quick Reaction Alert were held on special Operational Readiness Platforms adjacent to the main runways for a rapid take-off.

The V-Force was controlled from Bomber Command's Headquarters at

The UK detonated their first nuclear weapon, a plutonium atom bomb weighing 10,000lb (4,536kg) off North-Western Australia on 3 October 1952. This made them the third nation to join the nuclear powers after the US and the USSR

The weight of Britain's atomic bombs meant that the RAF's existing piston-engined Avro Lincoln bombers were unable to carry them. The answer was found in the creation of a jet-propelled V-Bomber force. First to enter service were the Valiants in 1955, followed by the Vulcans and Victors two years later. A prototype Avro Vulcan VX770 is shown above

High Wycombe, Bucks, through two subordinate Groups, Nos 1 and 3, based at Bawtry in South Yorkshire and Mildenhall in Suffolk. However, in times of tension or exercises, 26 dispersal airfields around the country were designated as temporary bases. Taking into account the ten main bases, 36 stations were available for housing the V-bombers.

Communication between the bases was vital. Their airfields were connected by private circuits and teleprinter lines provided by the GPO, later the Post Office Corporation (POC). In addition, the various commanders at HQ, Group and station level needed to be able to speak to the aircraft captain and other members of the crew, wherever they were, over secure telephone-type lines.

The Air Defence (AD) Group was given the task of designing a national broadcast system. Named Bomber Broadcast, the network used 4-wire private circuits connected in a ring configuration around the bases and dispersal airfields. High quality, low loss, private circuits amplified at intervals and routed over the GPO's national transmission network provided the core. The network was controlled from HQ Bomber Command with links to the Groups and airfields, but with the physical implementation of a ring structure. Feeder lines from the ring were dropped off at each station and headquarters and then connected by branching amplifiers to the Operational Readiness Platforms (ORPs).

A limited version of the network was installed in the early Sixties using a few private circuits and what were known as Hadley Teletalk boxes but the system was radically upgraded in the late 1960s by GPO engineer Tom Behan. He was asked to expand and modernise it and to overcome the problem of interference in the aircrews' headsets. Many old valve amplifiers in the original network were replaced by modern transistor units and new private circuits were added.

Tom had to address the problem of connecting what was effectively a telephone line into the bombers and making it compatible with the intercom circuit of the aircraft. He did it by using matching amplifiers and attenuators on the ground so that the telephone line appeared like another crew member to the intercom. Connection from the ground was by means of a 4-way jack plug and an umbilical cable connected to each ORP. The plug assembly – designed by another AD Group engineer, Wally Setchfield – was made self-releasing by the crew when, or shortly before, the bomber took off.

Trials to find out what was causing the headset interference problem were undertaken by Tom Behan at Boscombe Down in 1970. In a situation unique to a GPO engineer he was asked to sign and take responsibility for a Vulcan B.Mk1 bomber worth several million pounds. The RAF crew were complaining about interference in their headsets. He traced the fault to an unbalanced amplifier in the intercom circuit and quickly cured it by introducing a transformer in front of the amplifier, so that the modification worked without interfering with the aircraft's intercom and other systems. He then handed the aircraft back. Subsequently, all Vulcans and Victors were modified to incorporate Tom's transformer and nothing more was heard of cockpit interference.

The new Bomber Broadcast network was completed by 1972 and remained in service until the V-Force stood down in 1982.

Between 1945 and 1980, therefore, NATO had been born and had become the most powerful military alliance the world had ever seen. Britain had re-shaped and modernised her armed forces and had designed and equipped an air defence system capable of meeting all the demands of collective security. Meanwhile, in Germany, Russia's expansionist ambitions had been held in check by British and American forces. As always, communications had played a vital role.

---

1 The programming was by means of wire straps that marked the numbers required and made the key-sender dial the correct sequence of numbers.

PEACE AND COLD WAR IN GERMANY

Introduction

After the war, the Potzdam Conference agreed on the division of Germany into four zones, each controlled by one of the four principal members of the victorious allies. As soon as Montgomery's 21 Army Group had taken control, the Foreign Office became responsible for governing the British Zone in North West Germany. Representatives of the French, British, American and USSR governments made up the Control Commission Germany (CCG).

Germany went through a lengthy de-nazification process to ensure that there was no resurgence of nationalism. In addition, West Germany had to be reconstructed and groomed for sovereignty as a bulwark against Russian ambitions. With this in mind, each of the Western Powers, and particularly Britain, brought into Germany large numbers of experts. They included trades union officials, leading industrialists and skilled personnel from the electrical companies, railways, police, customs and post and telecommunications. The GPO featured largely in this operation.

Into war-devastated Germany came some 2,000 GPO staff, initially known as the Post & Telecommunications (P&T) Group, to provide telecommunications for the Control Commission Germany (CCG). This included the immense task of repairing the huge network of destroyed overhead telephone lines, a task also undertaken by Royal Signals personnel such as the BAOR line detachment shown here

The occupying powers played a major role in creating the new German constitution. Central government retained control of the Armed Forces, Foreign Policy, Highways and Posts and Telecommunications, but everything else was devolved to the "lande" or provinces. They could levy taxes and so were able to influence the way that resources were used.

Into a country devastated by war came about 2,000 people from the GPO. Initially they were called Post & Tele-communications (P&T) Group, but after Germany regained sovereignty in 1954 they were renamed TELS Group and worked not for the Foreign Office but for the War Office.

While restoring the country's telecommunications network, GPO staff also had to install special secure networks for the British forces. New 'parent' zone exchanges had to be installed and older existing military exchanges linked into them Switchboards were similar to the one shown, installed for 1(BR) Corps

Their first task was to provide tele-communications for the CCG. Nothing worked anywhere. Telephone lines had to be re-established, and voice frequency tele-graph and some control lines had to be provided for the exclusive use of the CCG and the armed forces. As 21 Army Group had their HQ near Minden in Westphalia and the RAF HQ was nearby at Bad Elsen, the zone telephone exchange needed to be

THE SOCIAL CALL SERVICE

In the late 1940s, telephones were still fairly exotic pieces of equipment to private soldiers in Germany. Most calls were made from public call boxes and inevitably there were queues. The GPO introduced the Social Call Service.

They suggested that the military made some of their lines available outside normal working hours for the soldiers to call home to their wives, girlfriends, mums and dads. The system worked like clockwork. Calls were booked well ahead and the GPO, which then manned the War Office switchboard in London, ensured that the British recipient was on the line at the right moment. In a different form, the Social Call Service has lasted to this day.

close to both and was installed, using GPO equipment, in a former Bank building in Minden.

Although many overhead lines had been destroyed, most of those underground survived. The rest were repaired and new cabling put in if necessary. The equipment was of the Strowger type, simple and similar to that used in the UK. But to create the discreet networks which were needed, new 'parent' zone exchanges had to be installed and the older barrack and airfield exchanges linked into them to separate them from the public telephone system. All costs were met by the German nation.

At the same time P&T Group were responsible for observing and sometimes supervising the employees of the German Post Office as they rebuilt the civilian communication networks. During the early postwar days, there were relatively few Reichspost staff. Hundreds of thousands of Germans were still in Russia, more were in North Africa, some were prisoners of war in Canada and Britain. Many who had been on active service were still undergoing the denazification process, along with others who had not been in uniform but in reserved occupations.

The process of rebuilding a communications network for the general public and a discreet network to support the CCG and the armed forces continued until West Germany became a sovereign nation in 1954, and the role of the CCG was over.

State of Forces Agreement

The CCG did not just walk away. They had to agree the status of the troops left behind in Germany and this was embodied in the State of Forces Agreement (SOFA) drawn up by the national governments, passed by their individual parliaments and lodged in Washington. It still exists. It covered every aspect of life and importantly, so far as telecommunications was concerned, guaranteed special rates for the lines or communications services which were rented from the German Bundespost and special rules for their provision.

The SOFA was amended three times – in 1959, 1979 and 1995. At the end of the Millennium, it is radically reduced in scale but in the past, the victorious nations were given great power. The British forces, for example, could exercise over any piece of land in West Germany; quite often they would drive tanks into farmyards and take over buildings and parts of towns. If a line of communication was needed between two points in Germany, the Bundespost was required to provide it within 48 hours, even if it meant depriving a civilian user. TELS Group would do all the liaison and ensure it was done.

In 1979 new telecommunications tariffs were agreed. Later, in 1995, the SOFA was renegotiated. The troops in Germany still have to be provided with the services they need. So far as telecommunications was concerned, Britain retained the right to choose between the normal public rates – which were coming down all the time – and the special rate which would be reduced by 20 per cent every year until 2001. After that no preferential rates would remain.

The Army now became responsible for providing all ground and static communications between and within the RAF airfields and wherever they were in the field. In 1968 this was maintained by 21 Signal Regiment.

The Signal Squadron is primarily manned by GPO/BT staff and BT has carried out extensive work to support 21 Signal Regiment, especially with the RAF in Germany.

In 1996, the whole telephone system and the radio relay STARRNET system were completely re-equipped with a system supplied by Northern Telecom. The maintenance element of the contract however was subject to a separate bid and TELS Division, part of 2 Signal Brigade, won on costs against competition from German Telecom, British Telecom and Northern Telecom. British Engineers therefore continue to maintain all the radio relay networks, satellite ground stations, including the new one at HQ Rheindahlen and the telephone exchanges.

AIR FORMATION SIGNALS

Between the two World Wars, a number of independent Signals Units were created to meet the needs of the Royal Air Force. They were known first as RAF Signals, Royal Corps of Signals, then as Air Contingent Signals and from 1937 as Air Formation Signals. During World War Two, 21,000 members of the Corps provided and maintained landline communications and a Despatch Rider Letter Service for the RAF.

After 1945 the role of Air Formation Signals did not change dramatically but the technology did. The Motorcycle Despatch Rider was replaced by multi-channel radio. Manual telephone exchanges were replaced by electro-mechanical, then electronic exchanges. Circuits now carry data as well as telegraph and voice.

While Air Formation Signals Units existed to provide ground communications for the RAF, Air Support Signals Units (ASSU) provided forward ground-to-air communications to co-ordinate air support for the Field Army.

During the 1960s, the term 'Air Formation' was replaced by 'Air Support.' Today the role of 21 Signal Regiment includes both Air Formation and Air Support functions.

THE TRANSISTOR*

from the TRANSfer of current across a resISTOR

Towards the end of World War Two, Melvin Kelly, Director of Research at the Bell Telephone Company's Laboratory, was looking for ways to increase the efficiency of telecommunications systems. His main aim was to improve the slow speed of electro-mechanical relays, and the reliability, power consumption and heat dissipation of thermionic valves. In the summer of 1945, a group investigated the feasibility of using semi-conductor technology when designing an amplifier. William Shockley, one of the leaders, began designing a semi-conductor replacement for the thermionic valve, helped by his colleagues William Brattain, 1902-1987, and John Bardeen.

In the early 1900s certain crystals had been found to act as rectifiers, but the group discovered that crystals of germanium and silicon with the right amount of impurity performed better. On 16 December 1947, using a thin layer of germanium with 'point-contact' needles touching the crystal – to which metal contacts were attached – they invented the point-contact transistor, which both rectified and amplified current.

The fundamental physics involved were not then understood, but by the end of January 1948, after studying the positive/negative (p-n) junction theory, Shockley had demonstrated the workings of the silicon junction transistor, in which a layer of lightly doped n-type material was sandwiched between two layers of p-type, or vice versa. This also rectified and amplified current.

Bell Labs had produced both types in small quantities early in 1951, but neither was thought suitable for large-scale manufacture. Production techniques were refined to produce point-contact transistors of reasonable quality. For the next ten years these were used by Western Electric in telephone equipment, hearing aids, and early digital computers.

It was found that silicon transistors performed better at room temperature, and had a higher melting point and a more critical chemical and metallurgical structure than germanium. Bell Labs obtained the necessary high-quality silicon by extracting silicon crystals comparable to the highest quality germanium from a melt contained in a silica 'boat'. In 1952, Bell Labs offered their transistor patents freely to other companies on payment of an initial royalty; rapid advances in the performance and manufacture of transistors followed. Shockley, Brattain and Bardeen jointly received the 1956 Nobel Prize for Physics in recognition of their pioneering work.

The initially heavy RAF commitment to Germany was considerably reduced by the Sandys Defence White Paper of 1957, from 33 squadrons to 12. During the 1970s these included Phantom F622s, Buccaneer S.2s, Harrier GR1s, Lightning F2s and a complete squadron of Wessex helicopters. A naval anti-submarine Wessex is shown here

The Royal Air Force in Germany

At the close of the Second World War in May 1945, the RAF had 36 operational squadrons in Germany. They formed the British Air Forces of Occupation (BAFO) and provided the fighter, fighter-reconnaissance, ground attack and technical support elements, based on eight former Luftwaffe airfields.

NATO was established on 1 April 1951, with headquarters in Paris, and BAFO were then reduced to a single group, re-named the 2nd Tactical Air Force (2TAF)and assigned to NATO's Supreme Allied Commander in Europe (SACEUR), General Dwight D Eisenhower. By the beginning of 1952, 2TAF comprised sixteen squadrons on five bases sited along the German border to maintain a watching brief on Soviet and East German forces.

Despite the end of the Berlin Airlift in May 1949, NATO remained deeply suspicious of Soviet intentions towards Europe. Forward basing policy changed and the RAF squadrons were moved further west of the Rhine.

In 1951 NATO's Medium Term Plan defined what forces were needed in Germany. As a result by the end of 1952, 2TAF was increased from 15 to 31 squadrons. Within a further two years, the number had grown to 56, a disproportionate number of which were light bombers operating in the offensive tactical nuclear strike role.

The size of the RAF commitment to Germany meant more airfields were needed. No 83 Group was recreated at Wahn and additional airfields were opened at Jever and Oldenburg. In 1954, new airfields at Bruggen, Geilenkirchen, Wildenrath and Laarbruch were completed, along with a new joint headquarters for the RAF and British Army of the Rhine at Rheindahlen, near Moenchengladbach. They were joined later by the headquarters of NATO's 2ATAF.

By 1957 air strength had reduced to 33 squadrons, but the infamous Sandys Defence White Paper of that year saw sixteen squadrons disbanded and the forward airfields, except Gutersloh, abandoned. No 83 Group was also closed. The 2TAF was re-named RAF Germany in 1959 and in 1961 a further six front-line squadrons were withdrawn. The remaining twelve were dispersed between Gutersloh and the four so-called "clutch" airfields at Bruggen, Laarbruch, Geilenkirchen and Wildenrath. In 1967 Geilenkirchen was returned to the Luftwaffe. After all these changes there was a period of stability.

During the early Seventies the four squadrons of Canberras were replaced by four Phantom F622 squadrons and two of Buccaneers. Two squadrons of Hunters were replaced by three squadrons of Harrier fighter reconnaissance GR1s. In addition there were two squadrons of Lightning F2s and one of Wessex helicopters. They were based on four airfields – Bruggen, Laarbruch, Gutersloh and Wildenrath.

The Airfield Survival Measures Programme

From 1974 onwards NATO implemented an Airfield Survival Measures Programme. which entailed RAF Germany building a series of "hardened" structures to protect their assets – buildings, communications and aircraft. These immensely tough buildings were capable of withstanding anything but a direct hit from a heavy bomb. The airfields were completely redesigned with the Combined Operations Centre (COC) as the focal point, designed to run the airfield in time of war. In turn the Operations Centre was connected to the headquarters of each squadron by cables routed around the airfield's perimeter away from likely targets for enemy attack. The Squadron's HQ was in turn provided with ring cables that interconnected a series of Hardened Aircraft Shelters for the squadron's aircraft. A standby COC was also established to provide backup command and control if the main Centre was hit. The hardened buildings were also fitted with systems to protect them from the effects of nuclear, chemical and biological (NBC) warfare. The airfield's lighter coloured "soft" structures – hangars, administration buildings and air traffic control tower – were camouflaged by the application of copious quantities of drab green paint, making them very difficult to see from the air especially when travelling at high speed.

Before this, communications on RAF airfields in Germany had been provided by key and lamp unit systems, installed after the Second World War. By the early Seventies they all needed replacing with something more compact and easier to maintain. This ruled out conventional hard wired systems, as the operators now had to wear full NCB suits and respirators which did not allow them the dexterity to repair faults, mend broken wires, or replace failed bulbs. Something akin to the idea of line replaceable units, then being introduced in the RAF's Harrier and Jaguar aircraft would be required.

The space inside the hardened buildings was considerably less than that in previous RAF buildings, so the new series of communications equipments which AD Group was invited to design and build would have to be smaller. Engineer Richard Howe and his assistant Graham Saville were given the design brief and, having established the initial requirement, a specification was produced in the autumn of 1973. Early in 1974 a design was completed and tested. Production was undertaken by a number of small specialist contractors, the systems were assembled and tested by the POC Team in London and were then flown out to Germany via the RAF's supply network. Training of technicians from 21 Signal Regiment was initially undertaken in London. They then returned to Germany with installation specifications, support documents and spares packs that would enable them to maintain the equipment. Towards the end of the first phase, personnel from 81 Signal Squadron became involved and they were trained on-site by Graham Saville.

By mid-1976 the first phase to provide a basic communications fit at each airfield was completed and POC set about expanding the system across all German airfields. Crash alarm systems were also installed in the Air Traffic Control Towers and other communications were provided for the movement of ordnance around the airfield and for RAF security staff. Finally, liquid crystal display clocks were developed in 1976, alongside transistor control circuits, to give accurate digital time displays.

This was the beginning of a long and fruitful relationship between the POC Air Defence Group, the officers and men of the Regiment's Airfield Communications Planning Office and the Signal Troops on the four German Airfields. The association lasted until RAF Germany closed down in the late 1990s.

As in the UK, RAF Germany planning staff began to upgrade their airfields in the latter part of the Eighties. This work concentrated on the replacement of the copper ring cables with ones in fibre optic, to provide digital services around airfields and achieve some commonality with RAF supply and logistical computer systems. Fibre optics offered considerable increases in the carrying capacities of the cables and an increase in the types of facilities that could be provided, including 64 Kbit/s speech, data services between 64 Kbit/s and 8 or 34 Mbit/s, and real-time video and computer graphics, still then in their infancy.

Fibre optic cables are difficult to lay and splice in battle damage repair conditions. They are also prone to increases in opaqueness in the presence of gamma rays produced by tactical nuclear weapons. However, BT's scientists and engineers at the Research Laboratories in Martlesham Heath, led by Mick Reeve, devised a system of blowing fibres through narrow tubes, which were in turn gathered together in cable-like bundles. Using standard compressors and specially prepared lengths of fibre, it was possible to blow in 500 metre, later extended to 1,000 metre, sections of fibre without recourse to splicing. Since buildings on airfields were rarely more than a kilometre apart, no splicing would be required. The opacity problem was ignored, for if the cables were affected by nuclear radiation, the same would apply to personnel, and the airfield would no longer be operational!

Trial sections of blown fibre cable were installed at Bruggen by personnel from 21 Signal Regiment under the supervision of engineers Steve Marsden and Roger Clarke from Martlesham in 1988, when a section of the airfield ring cable was replicated in fibre, but lack of funds and the end of the Cold War in 1989 precluded the need for further developments.

The MoD's 'Options for Change' of July 1990 halved the strength of the RAF in Germany and reduced it from an independent command to a subordinate Group, No 2, reporting to the AOC-in-C Strike Command. In 1992 the bases at Wildenrath and Gutersloh were closed and their squadrons disbanded, or transferred to Laarbruch. This move was a preliminary to the closure, after nearly 50 years, of all RAF bases in Germany during the late 1990s.

History of 81 Signal Squadron 1924-1999

The origins of 81 Signal Squadron can be traced to the formation of 1 Kite Balloon Signal Section in Leeds, when the Supplementary Reserve was created in 1924. Five years later, the Section was expanded and re-named No. 3 (West Riding) Company, Line of Communication Signals.

In 1935, the Unit expanded again and was converted into Royal Air Force Signals. It had a headquarters and four companies, two in Leeds, one in London and one in Birmingham. In 1936 it was renamed Air Contingent Signals and in 1938 Air Formation Signals (AFS).

The Unit's function was to provide landlines and despatch rider communications for the Air Component of the Army's Expeditionary Force – later the British Expeditionary Force in France – in the event of war. During May 1939, a new unit was urgently formed to provide communications for the RAF's Advanced Air Striking Force (AASF).

Shortly after the outbreak of war in September 1939, both units, now the 1 and 2 AFS, were mobilised and despatched to France. Their experience with the RAF until the evacuation of the British Expeditionary Force in June 1940 proved valuable for the future. Following their return to the UK, both Units were employed with the RAF in various capacities during the Battle of Britain and the preparations to repel an invasion during August and September 1940.

At the end of 1942, both units were posted to North Africa to participate in Operation TORCH and subsequently served throughout the Italian Campaign. The 1st AFS were allocated to HQ Allied Air Forces Mediterranean and the 2nd to Mediterranean Allied Coastal Air Force. During these operations, 2 AFS became widely dispersed. At one time the unit's various companies were some 1,000 miles apart.

At the end of the war, both units were disbanded but with the formation of the Army Emergency Reserve (AER) in 1950, 50 AFS Regiment AER was raised at Chester from the core of the old two units. In 1953, the Regiment carried out their annual training with 11 Air Formation Signals Regiment in Germany. They were the first non-regular unit to do so. In 1956 and 1960, the Regiment returned to Germany to train with regular AFS regiments.

During 1960, the unit was re-named 81 Signal Regiment and was amalgamated the following year with 90 Signal Regiment. Under the new organisation, the Regiment's No 1 Squadron was given a call up commitment under a Category 1 of the AER and earmarked for a Far East support role.

Overseas training became a regular feature and included visits to Germany in 1962, 1963 and 1966. Small detachments also helped the regular army in Aden with permanent fixed communications.

When the Reserve Army was re-organised in 1967, 81 Signal Regiment (Volunteers) amalgamated with 66 (Ulster) Signal Regiment (V) to form 40 Signal Regiment (V). After two years as a squadron of the 40th in Ulster, the unit became an independently sponsored unit as 81 Signal Squadron (V), with headquarters moving to Middlesbrough to enable them to be administered by 34 Signal Regiment (V).

Over the next fifteen years, 1970–1985, the Squadron trained for a war role, reinforcing their Regular sister Unit No 3 Squadron of 21 Signal Regiment (Air Support), and providing ground communications support to the squadrons and bases of RAF Germany. Throughout this period 81 Signal Squadron camped every year at RAF stations Laarbruch, Bruggen, Wildenrath and Gutersloh. During this time the GPO and later British Telecom, were again involved, designing and maintaining equipment for the airfield survival measures programme.

After the re-unification of Germany in 1990, the whole structure of British

Forces came under review in "Options for Change" and 81 Signal Squadron joined with 43 Signal Squadron (V), 220 Signal Squadron and 244 Signal Squadron to become the constituent parts of a new 21 Signal Regiment (Air Support). As a result, the Squadron became part of one of the first fully integrated Regular/TA units in the British Army. In July 1999, as part of the MoD's Strategic Defence Review, 81 Signal Squadron left 21 Signal Regiment to become an independent squadron within 2 Signal Brigade, tasked with the provision of fixed communications.

EMD and STARRNET

Until the mid 1960s, Strowger pre-war designed equipment was still being made by the Siemens and ATV companies, but because of the enormous damage caused to the German telephone network during the war which had been restored to working order but not modernised, TELS Liaison Group decided to install a modern German-made system called EMD (Electromechanical Motor Driven).. It was based on motor driven switches and gold plated contacts. The advantages were speed and silent operation; it was in a sense the Rolls-Royce of electrical telephone exchanges at the time. The Germans designed a special EMD relay set for TELS Group which could be used for either single or bi-directional connections. It was the first time that the Group had been involved in something which was State of the Art and was the

Until the mid 1960s, Strowger pre-war designed equipment – similar to that used in the UK – was still available, but to create the secure networks essential for the military, the GPO TELS Liaison Group in Germany decided to adopt the faster, more efficient modern German EMD – Electromechanical Motor Driven – system. It was used with the Siemens Rhine Army 1954 switchboard which could be used on the move, as in this BAOR teleprinter vehicle

biggest change in fixed military communications in Germany since the war.

There had been other changes. In 1954 Siemens had designed the RA54 (Rhine Army 1954) switchboard for the British Army and it was used throughout the private telephone network in Germany and in the back of vehicles. The RAF had a small radio-relay system interconnecting the clutch airfields of Hildenrat, Laarbruck and Bruggen (the term clutch was used because they were covered by the Dusseldorf Clutch Radar System). The Army relied on rented lines of communication. At DM12 per month per km, it was not expensive, but with over a thousand lines there was a need not only to save money but to provide secure speech. The Static Radio Relay Network (STARRNET) system was the result. The Army quickly welcomed the suggestion put forward by the Group, now working under the Commander Royal Signals Germany, that a new radio relay system should be put in place which would pay for itself and provide secure speech between the HQ at Moenchengladbach and BR

RISTACOM AND COMCAN

After World War Two, the Army Wireless Chain expanded to include a number of Commonwealth countries. COMCAN (Commonwealth Communications Army Network) had grown by the late 1960s into an intricate network of HF sys-

tems. The Army had a High Frequency system linking the UK to Canada, Australia, West Africa, Cyprus, Malta, India, Hong Kong and Singapore. The RAF had a similar system which linked Britain with Australia, Hong Kong, and Cyprus. The Navy operated yet another parallel system. Rationalisation was needed.

Under the RISTACOM agreement in the late 1960s, it was decided that the RAF would become responsible for long haul communications including the first military Satellite, SKYNET 1. The RAF would also look after long haul telegraph communications. RISTACOM – Rationalisation of Inter Services Telecommunications – was an influential landmark in the story of fixed military communications.

Under the RISTACOM agreement in the late 1960s, the RAF took responsibility for the first military satellite, SKYNET 1. The Army provided all ground and static communications between and within the RAF airfields and wherever planes were in the field. This photograph of 14 Signal Regiment's mobile satellite-communications station was taken in 1969

Corps.

At that time, most of the communications group still came from the GPO. STARRNET was therefore effectively conceived and designed by GPO Engineers in Germany who let the contract to Marconi Italiana. It came into being in 1969 and stretched from Birgelin right against the Dutch border to Hannover in the north via Bielefeld, BR Corps HQ and incorporated the existing RAF net. The 56-channel system was arranged in a herringbone pattern across the whole area of operations in Germany.

The system had to be maintained solely by British personnel. This was especially important at the time because there were said to be 20,000 spies in West Germany employed in all walks of life. It was thought that twelve engineers would be needed spread over three or four teams and they would be responsible for maintaining the network 24 hours a day.

This was where problems were encountered. Until that time there had never been a problem in recruiting from the GPO. But in the late 1960s, it was different. GPO salaries were racing ahead of those on offer in Germany. The answer came unexpectedly from the changes generated by the RISTACOM agreement.

The recruiting spotlight was turned around and all twelve engineers needed for STARRNET were recruited from COMCAN. By April 1969, the system was up and running.

One of those COMCAN engineers was Ben Morgan. He joined the Telecommunications Group in 1968 working to 4 Signal Brigade, and remained with

Ben Morgan

the organisation until his retirement in 1998. Working initially as an engineer on STARRNET, he became Manager of the Regional offices of the Group at Bielefeld. From 1984 he headed TELS Division – which he re-named to give it an identity within 4 Signal Brigade, and from 1985 onwards, chaired the State of Forces Working Group on Communications. He was awarded the OBE for his services to the British Armed Forces.

"By 1968 the size of the Group had reduced to something like 29 people. They were all without exception from the British GPO. That was the point when they were told that they had to go back to the GPO or transfer permanently to the MoD. Nearly all of them stayed. They were joined by the twelve engineers, of which I was one, from COMCAN. The group then increased again up to 65 or 66 British engineers, and there was still a good sprinkling of GPO among them. And that is still the case today."

By 1972, the STARRNET system had grown to the point where a full STD system could be introduced across the military network in Germany. Using tropospheric scatter, STD could also be provided across the Channel and into the UK networks.

Ben Morgan takes up the story again:

"In those days international circuits always went through an international exchange. There was an agreed interchange point between two countries – sometimes in the ether – and it was closely monitored under international specifications and regulation. A different system governed the operation of the international circuits from Germany to England used by the military. The British military system in the UK was slightly different from that in Germany and the two had to be connected by using a tropospheric scatter system which was not easy to use.

There was a vital need for close co-operation between those who maintained the exchanges in Germany and 2 Signal Brigade and the GPO who maintained the exchanges in England. BT were not allowed to talk to the Germans so we, the military users, had to provide the liaison. I represented the British military in Germany, and Jack Hendry was Telecommunications Traffic Superintendent (TTS) on secondment from the GPO to the Army in UK.

We used to meet in the old BT telephone exchange in High Holborn. Jack Hendry later came over to Germany and became Head of the Telecommunications Group in 1983, my immediate predecessor".

Modernisation gathers pace

It was time now to go digital. TELS Division examined what was available in Germany which would work to German standards and provide an ISDN service. Colonel Roger Thompson, now retired, commanded TELS Division from 1986 and remembers the enormous changes in communication which he saw during the late 1980s:

"Between the mid 1970s and 1990, everything changed. Thermionic valves gave way to transistors and semi-conductors. The communications revolution resulted in the end of TELS Division as it had been before. The work was no longer needed. By the time I left Germany in 1990, you were putting equipment which had needed a whole building into a smallish box. The new equipment needed little or no maintenance; if something went wrong, you just took one little bit out and put another little bit in. We no longer needed the hundreds of people on the road to maintain the kit. Diagnostic equipment could be run by just one person and he would be able instantly to find out just where to find just where to locate the bit of equipment he needed. All this happened in about two years".

THE FALKLANDS WAR

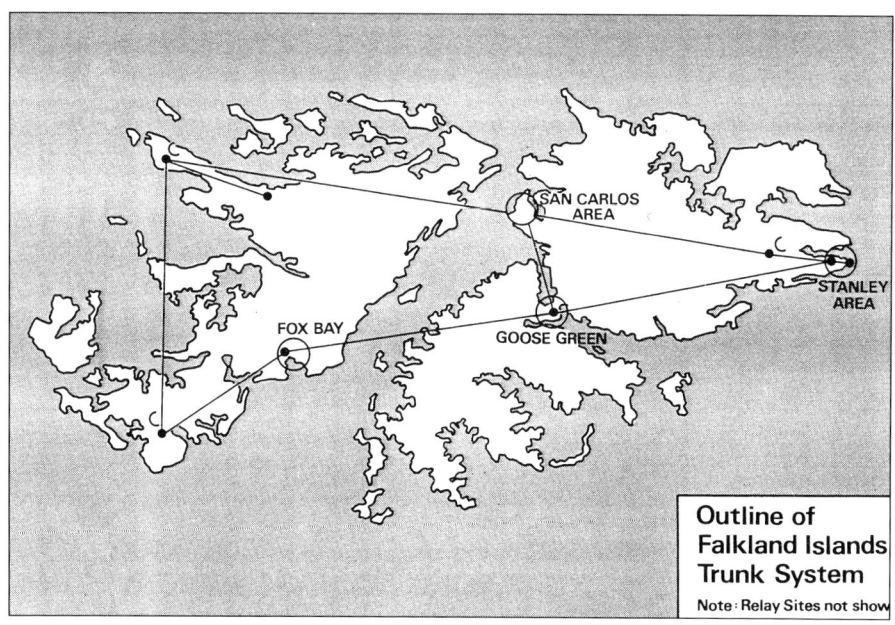

The Falkland Islands and the battle to recapture them dominated the world press and the minds of the British people in the spring and summer months of 1982. For the first time in twenty years, a British military force had been called upon to use the full weight of modern fire power to eject an enemy which had illegally attacked and occupied British territory.

On 2 April 1982, Argentine Forces invaded and occupied the British Colony of the Falkland Islands. The military Junta controlling Argentina at the time believed that Britain would not retaliate. They were encouraged in this belief by the announcement a few weeks earlier that the British government was permanently to withdraw the survey ship HMS *Endurance* from the South Atlantic. They were wrong.

Within three days, a Task Force of 30 ships and two aircraft carriers had left Portsmouth on 5 April. Initial elements included HMS *Hermes* and HMS *Invincible*

Following the invasion of the Falkland Islands by Argentine forces on 2 April 1982, a UK Task Force of 30 ships and two aircraft carriers sailed from Portsmouth within three days. Among them were HMS Hermes, *above, shown with RAF Sea Harriers on her deck, and HMS* Broadsword, *in the background.*

with 3 Commando Brigade, a Parachute Battalion and all supporting arms. HMS *Fearless* sailed 24 hours alter. The number was to rise to an incredible 110 vessels. British submarines had been dispatched ahead. An educational cruise liner, the *Uganda*, was converted into a hospital ship. The 45,000 ton cruise ship *Canberra* was converted into a troop ship and in addition to 2,000 Marines and Paras, carried helicopters, munitions and stores. It was an extraordinary logistic exercise, rarely equalled before.

When the Falklands crisis broke, Dave Spring was Engineer in Charge of the Army Telephone Network and the main point of contact between the Army and Post Office Communications. At the time, monthly meetings were held with the Army to discuss "fluid" jobs – orders which were being placed but had not yet been implemented. One of these fluid projects was a circuit network between the ATN and British Rail so that the Army could notify British Rail when and where they needed a train for a specific purpose. The Railways had been dragging their feet for a long time and the project had become a regular fixture on the monthly meeting agenda.

On the Monday after the debate in Parliament and Mrs Thatcher's speech, British Rail contacted BT. Where was the circuit? They were politely told why it was not in place. Plugs were pulled out and the network was in place and operating by Thursday morning.

Ascension Island was the launching pad. Communications troops, logistic and combat supplies were rapidly moved south ready to support the build up of the Task Force. Fully secure speech and telegraph communications from Ascension to the United Kingdom were vital at this stage to facilitate political direction, the huge build up of logistic supplies and to prepare for the arrival of additional forces leapfrogging

HMS Fearless, *above, set sail 24 hours after the main naval contingent. They were to rendezvous at Ascension Island, where additional forces had already arrived by air, and fully secure speech and telegraph communications back to the UK had been set up by 30 Signal Regiment*

the ship-borne Task Force. The communications centre and strategic rear link troops were therefore part of the first elements to leave the United Kingdom and enter what was to become the War Zone. Men from 30 Signal Regiment operated a mixture of military and civilian equipment to provide rear link communications,

As the spearhead elements forged south, it was essential to improve the secure communications required within the United Kingdom. The special trunk communications squadron of 30 Signal Regiment was deployed to link the principal operational and supporting headquarters in the United Kingdom with the ports of embarkation, logistic depots and main strategic air bases.

By the time the Task Force had landed at San Carlos, Post Office Liaison Officer Ian White, seconded to Communications Projects Division, School of Signals, was already involved in the Falklands communications planning and had been asked to undertake responsibility for all static (fixed) cable planning on the Islands after the conflict. Dave Spring was in a different group tasked with providing standard BT equipment where and when needed. During the conflict there was a great deal of increased activity to enhance the existing network and adding circuits to cope with the additional traffic. Circuits between various military networks had to be provided very quickly and much overtime was needed.

"One day I had a phone call from my opposite number in 2 Signals Group asking if they could have more circuits in the Barracks by Buckingham Palace. He couldn't tell me more but just asked me to watch the television at 4pm that afternoon when the lugubrious MoD spokesman Ian MacDonald used to give regular updates on what was happening. That afternoon he reported a serious incident involving the Welsh Guards who had been trapped on board the LSL Sir Galahad *which had been bombed by the Argentinians. Before the day was over, the connection to the main Army Network at Wellington Barracks was congested because everyone was phoning to find out what was happening."*

This vivid painting by Peter Archer shows 30 Signal Regiment at San Carlos Bay during the retaking of the Falklands. Signallers are shown with Satellite Communications (SATCOM) equipment and the Maritime Rear Link (MRL). They had to work fast to provide secure circuits between the various military networks and back to the UK

After the conflict

Few communications facilities had existed in the Islands before the war, and those which did exist had been either destroyed or damaged. The immediate restitution of a telephone system in Port Stanley was vital for the administration of the capital by the civil and military commissioners and their staff. It was urgent to establish a new Garrison Headquarters with radio and telephone communications within the islands and secure speech and telegraph communication back to the United Kingdom.

In early July, a Youth Hostel and an old school were taken over for the Headquarters of the British Forces in the Falklands and the satellite was established for the third time. By now, the weather had worsened and almost every day it was necessary to climb up and adjust the antennae. The bitter cold and high winds on Stanley Airfield replaced the Argentines as the main enemy.

By August 1982, a month after the enemy's final surrender, the Antarctic winter had taken hold and flying was restricted to a few hours each week.

Planning for the future – post-conflict communications on the Falklands 1982-1984

With the Islands secure, British forces had their headquarters and air support based in and around Stanley. Tactical air defence radars were quickly set up in the hills surrounding the town, a logistical centre was established at San Carlos followed by garrisons at Goose Green and Fox Bay. A detachment of RAF Harriers was also based on Goose Green to provide a forward air defence capability. Other than the Island's civilian VHF radio, little in the way of communications was available to support these centres.

Once the conflict was over, the British forces' headquarters at Stanley had to be linked with the logistical centre at San Carlos, garrisons at Goose Green and Fox Bay and the detachment of RAF Harriers. A small interim military network was set up with Triffid radio equipment, Bruin telephone exchanges and, in the field, networks using Clansman portable radios, tested in the Falklands for the first time

To overcome this problem, a small interim military network was quickly set up. It comprised Triffid radio equipment, Bruin telephone exchanges and, in the field, Clansman radio networks. Because of the rudimentary nature of this network, frequent maintenance was required, and a large number of technicians were involved. Bearing in mind the distances concerned, this all took up a considerable amount of time and effort. In particular, the manning of hill-top sites for the Clansman broadcast sites and the Triffid radio relays produced a heavy logistical load. Communications to the UK were by the tactical satellite link, backed up by RAF high frequency equipment. Existing Cable & Wireless HF equipment had been put out of action during the fighting.

Once this rudimentary network was deployed, the MoD set about the task of planning a permanent network capable of handling the garrison, naval and air defence needs. The expertise for the installation of fixed cable communications on military airfields resided with RAF Germany's 21 (Air Support) Signal Regiment, whilst that for fixed telecommunications radio networks was the responsibility of the Communication Projects Agency of the School of Signals at Blandford in Dorset. Between them, these two units had to design and instal a temporary cable network on Stanley Airfield, plan a permanent one on a new airfield on Mount Pleasant and provide an islands-wide radio-relay network.

To help restore communications on the Islands, the UK MoD sent 30 Signal Regiment's senior airfield planner, WO2 FoS David Bowers, to assess conditions in Stanley Town and on the Airfield, to see if a small cable network could be centred on the control tower, and whether the airfield could be linked to the town by cable. The runway also needed clearing, as it was littered with wreckage such as the crashed Pucara aircraft in this photograph

Provision of Temporary Communications on Stanley Airfield

Before the war ended, Signal Regiment's senior airfield planner, Warrant Officer (WO2) Foreman of Signals (FoS) David Bowers was briefed at the MoD to travel down to the Islands and establish:

- What degree of damage had been suffered by the telephone and cable network within Stanley Town;
- How far it could be expanded to support the troops in the area;
- Whether a small cable network centred on the air traffic control tower could be built on Stanley Airfield;
- Whether it was feasible to link the Town to the Airfield by cable.

Dave Bowers arrived in the Falklands on 14 June 1982, the day the Argentinian forces surrendered. He quickly confirmed that the elderly civilian manual telephone exchange was in working order, as was the local cable distribution network, but neither could be expanded to support the Army Garrison and the RAF. It became clear the building of a civilian standard telephone network was beyond the capability of military personnel. They did not have the resources. The cost of handing this, essentially non-operational, work over to civilian contractors was prohibitively expensive and the requirement was dropped.

Having dealt with the town's cable network, Bowers turned his attention to the requirements of the airfield, situated to the east and connected to the town by a narrow strip of land – the Canache – not more than half a mile (800 metres) wide. He confirmed that an RAF-Germany style small airfield communications network, with a Combined Operations Centre located in the control tower, could be provided as part of the expansion needed to accommodate more sophisticated aircraft.

While the Harrier GR3s could fulfil this requirement in the short term, the RAF needed a longer runway for the Phantom FGR2s in the air defence role. To meet this need, the RE lengthened the runway at the small civilian airfield just outside the town on East Falkland by laying down sections of temporary runway plating made from a high impact fibre composite material. Runway arrestor gear was installed at one end to enable the Phantoms to land carrier-style. By a happy coincidence the Phantom was designed as a fleet defence fighter capable of operating from an aircraft carrier and came provided with an arrestor hook!

The work involved in the design, planning and installation of a proper airfield cable network would take too long and an interim solution was required to enable the aircraft to operate safely. A short-term solution was adopted by the laying down of a network using standard Army field cable, quantities of which were readily available in the UK and Germany. The main drawback was the constant maintenance required. The weather conditions in the Falklands meant that if the cable connectors got wet – a not infrequent occurrence – they would fail. A Heath-Robinson remedy was developed in the Line Section of the School of Signals whereby the connectors and the first

few inches of cable either side were wrapped in self amalgamating tape to provide a watertight seal. It was tested by immersion in a bucket of water. The "bodge" worked well and the seal remained watertight.

On his return to the UK, Dave Bowers submitted a proposal for the cable works on Stanley Airfield to connect the Air Traffic Control tower via a sub-

The fully armed Phantom FGR2 shown here outside the rubber hangars on Stanley Airfield, shows the drop tanks fitted for long distance patrols and the AIM-9L Sidewinder air-to-air missiles under the wings

Triffid radio equipment formed part of the small interim military network which was set up on the Islands immediately following the conflict

marine cable to the Cable and Wireless earth station; at the same time the airfield should be connected to Headquarters British Forces Falkland Islands in the old school buildings on the outskirts of Stanley Town. The MoD accepted his recommendations but the promise of a new airfield on Mount Pleasant avoided the need for other cable projects.

Dave Bowers was due to leave the Army in October 1982 and a replacement was needed to continue his work. Ian White, the Royal Signals Post Office Liaison Officer (POLO), an engineer on secondment to the Communications Projects Division at the School of Signals, was already involved in the Falklands communications planning. He was asked to take over the responsibility for planning the permanent network on Stanley Airfield. Ian's responsibility was later extended to include all static (fixed) cable planning in the Falkland Islands Theatre of Operations, including new airfields at Mount Pleasant, Ascension Island and South Georgia. To help him, MoD Army agreed to the posting of a senior NCO, Warrant Officer Tom Hornby, to the CPA in July 1982.

Before any design work on the cable network could begin, conditions on the islands had to be assessed. Little data existed on the weather, geological and logistical conditions other than that provided by David Bowers and other Royal Signals personnel on the Islands (mainly 30 Signal Regiment).

Eventually it was agreed that the shallowness of the soil in some parts and the exposure of hard rock meant that conventional underground cabling techniques would have to be modified. For example, consideration was given to running the cable on posts above the ground, as they are in the London Underground. This approach proved to be unnecessary as most cables could be laid in trenches dug into the ground. When hard rock was encountered, blasting by the RE quickly provided a route.

With these objectives in mind, Ian White and Tom Hornby began the detailed planning of the permanent network in January 1983. They were helped by the Property Services Agency and by the External Lineplant Division of Post Office Tele-

communications Headquarters. The first design was completed by March for comment by the MoD. As refinements and changes to the requirement were made, amendments were needed through the months of April and May and into June. There was a need to complete the installation during the Falklands summer and the cable and stores had to be on the islands by September/October 1983. The design was 'frozen' at that point to allow Ian White and Tom Hornby to estimate and cost the project.

The timescales were met in time and a party from 21 Signal Regiment, under the leadership of Sergeant Geoff Shipton, collected their stores on the Islands and began their work. Time was lost when some of the stores were 'appropriated' and later moved to a secure store, but after that things moved on quickly. With help from the resident detachment of the Regiment, the two 100-pair ring cables were laid and jointed by the end of January 1984. After that the team cabled out the dispersals, Air Traffic Control, rubber

Royal Signals Post Office Liaison Officer Ian White, seconded to Communications Projects Division, School of Signals, was tasked with responsibility for all post-conflict static (fixed) cable planning on the Islands, including the permanent network on Stanley Airfield, as well as new airfields at Mount Pleasant, Ascension Island and South Georgia hangars, ground defences and air defence Rapier units. The network was completed and commissioned for service in March 1984.

While all this work was going on, the *Herald* system in the Control Tower was replaced by a *Monarch* digital telephone switch installed by a team from the CPA to meet the airfield's increasing demand for telephones.

By March 1984, Stanley Airfield, or RAF Stanley as it had been named earlier, was equipped with a fully NATO standard airfield cable network to support all the operations of an RAF flying station.

The provision of a Submarine Cable

After the end of the War there were large numbers of aircraft and helicopters in and around Stanley Airfield. Facilities were cramped, so the Army's Scout helicopters were moved to Lookout Camp to the east of Stanley Town and the Search and Rescue helicopters were deployed to a location on the other side of Stanley Harbour on a piece of land named Navy Point. In order to provide communications to the Search and Rescue Flight it was proposed that a short range point to point radio relay link be set up across the harbour and connected, via a landline cable, to the Combined Operations Centre in the control tower. Even though the planned route of this link was outside the berthing area for shipping, it was not impossible that ships might be anchored there and there was the possibility that the link might be disconnected when ships passed or anchored in front of it, so isolating the helicopters when communication to Navy Point was lost.

The solution was seen to be a cross-harbour submarine cable, and Ian White was asked to investigate the feasibility of the Army laying a shallow-depth cable across the upper part of the harbour – a distance of some 1.25 miles/2km. Ian White and Major Martin from MoD Army visited the Branch's base at Southampton for a briefing on how to set about laying the cable and to establish what specialist equipment would be needed. The maritime engineers explained the sequence by which the cable should be prepared on board ship, described the necessary rollers and other specialist equipment and highlighted the safely rules when laying cable at sea. Drawings were provided so that all the necessary rollers and brackets could be fabricated by Royal Navy artificers.

The idea proved feasible, and the cable was obtained from the Post Office's Maritime Branch stores at Donibristle, near Dunfermline. In the spirit of a national emergency the Post Office agreed to the sale of two lengths of cable and their steel drums, each of which weighed over 10 tons (10.16 tonnes), at a modest price. No contract was signed; there was only a gentleman's agreement that if the account was rendered to the Army, the bill would be paid! A rather amusing story is linked to the payment of the bill. As agreed the bill was sent to the Army Department at the Ministry but when the clerk received it, he thought that as the money demanded was for something related to submarines, it was more appropriate that the Navy Department should pay for it. For their part the Navy knew nothing of the agreement and the bill shuffled between the two departments for a while until Major Martin heard about it, stopped the buck being passed and made the Army pay up!

Ian White wrote the instructions and safety measures required for laying the cable (best done at slack tide). It was successfully laid by No. 266 Signal Squadron under the command of Major, later Colonel, Bob Stark, Royal Signals, of the Joint Signals Staff as were the field cables to Moody Brook, all on a single day in October 1983.

The whole exercise was filmed for posterity; it was the first occasion that an Army Unit had laid submarine cable across such a large expanse of water. The cables remain in use to this day.

Inter-Island Communications

The problem of communications between the Islands, however, could not be solved by cabling, as the terrain was too rough and weather conditions too poor. Radio relay was the only viable option. Planning began during August 1982 when Dave Bowers was once again sent south to survey the cables linking the radio relay sites to the telephone exchanges and multiplexers and to assess the feasibility of laying a fibre optic cable from Stanley to Mount Pleasant. The link had to include the Army garrisons at Goose Green and Fox Bay; the RAF radar stations on East and West Falkland; the new strategic airfield on Mount Pleasant; HQ British Forces Falkland Islands; a new joint HQ; and the various logistical elements, including the Chinook helicopters in the San Carlos area.

In September 1982 a permanent planning team was set up at the CPA under Major, later Lieutenant Colonel, James Sweetman, Royal Signals. Ian White assumed responsibility for assessing helicopter lift requirements as well as looking after the cabling. The requirement now, following proposed cuts in manpower and logistical support, was for new, less manpower intensive systems. A new radio relay network was called for, known as the Falklands Islands Trunk System. The plans, completed by February 1983, involved the use of fibre optic cable, and positioning the weather-proof radio relay stations on hilltop sites. The position of only one of these had to be changed; a mapping inaccuracy had ignored a major obstacle in a radio path. The existence of this obstacle was established by Major Stark using binoculars at one end of the link and a helicopter hovering some ten feet above the ground many miles away with its lights on. It could not be seen. Fuel tanks were designed to be regularly replaced by Chinook helicopters; this was the main operating cost.

Marconi were awarded a contract in June 1983 and in the middle of the Falklands winter a combined team from Marconi and the Communications Projects Agency undertook a detailed survey which resulted in the choice of sites. The microwave system deployed was fully digital – 8 Mbit/s – to provide good speech quality for 120 x 64 Kbit/s channels. In practice only 60 channels were used on a day to day basis to provide spare capacity for re-routing purposes. To achieve a speedy turn round, off-the-shelf equipment was deliberately chosen by the MoD and a few strings had to be pulled to obtain some of the items.

The Post Office Corporation notably agreed to the Army being given priority for the supply of multiplexers ahead of other long established orders. Overall, industry responded well to the urgency of the project.

The trunk network on the Falkland Islands is monitored by a master computer in the Islands system control, from which it constantly monitors the network in alternative directions. The system control also acts as the engineering control for all circuits connected to the satellite and HF links, and monitors the digital telephone exchanges around the Islands. Installation of the trunk system began during April 1984. Two teams from the CPA installed the microwave equipment, and cable laying teams from Germany and the UK laid and terminated the multi-pair cables. By December, all sites had been completed. The system was commissioned and handed over to the Islands' Signals Squadron just 17 months and five days from the contract award.

The completion of the trunk network enabled the Army to remove all the tactical radio relay equipment from the Falklands, and to reduce the manning of No. 266 Signal Squadron by 80 men. In manpower costs alone, it was estimated that the system paid for itself within the first eighteen months of operation.

The Strategic Airfield at Mount Pleasant

It was always intended by the MoD that the airfield at Stanley would provide a temporary solution to the air defence problem and that a larger, more permanent base would be needed to support a British garrison. The new "strategic" airfield had to be capable of providing a base for a wide variety of RAF and civil aircraft; fighters for air defence, Harriers for the close air support of the Falklands Garrison in the event of the Argentineans attempting another invasion, long range transport aircraft for the resupply and the movement of troops and other service and civilian personnel, air refuelling tankers and helicopters for tactical lift and search and rescue. The site chosen for the airfield was a large plateau to the north-west of Stanley Town adjacent to

Mount Pleasant.

The new airfield was to be built to RAF Germany standards wherever possible in order that it might provide the best possible resilience against air attack:-

- A single main runway with alternative secondary runway capable of operating air defence fighters in an emergency.
- Full standard ring cabling around the runways and dispersals.
- Provision of emergency telephones in fuel and ammunition dumps.
- Connection to the trunk network and a new British Forces HQ.
- Connection to off-island communications at the Cable and Wireless earth station and RAF high frequency radio links.
- Connection to the naval facility at Mare Harbour.

A considerable number of RAF and Army personnel were to be accommodated on the airfield and would require the services of a telephone exchange with a linked number scheme connected to the Island's speech network by radio links.

The Formation of a Tri-Service Airfield Planning Team – Summer 1983

At the beginning of the airfield programme (Spring/Summer of 1983) officers and NCOs from all three services were formed into a loose team to front their branch's requirements in the overall design. Ian White was chosen as technical authority to lead the cable design aspects and given complete responsibility to design, plan and cost the installation. Once again, Ian was the only civilian member of an otherwise all service team.

Ian and Tom Hornby set about the task of the detailed communications cable design once the Property Services Agency had supplied them with outline drawings of the airfield and its buildings. Overall, the design took many drafts and four months to complete, before it could be forwarded to the MoD for approval and procurement action. The ground on and around Mount Pleasant was not known with any certainty, neither was the difficulty likely to be encountered with the digging of trenches and the laying of duct and cable. In order that these parameters might be established it was agreed that Ian would accompany Major Sweetman on his next visit to the Islands in late January 1984.

The survey undertaken with the co-operation of the staff of the Commander Communications, Falkland Islands, Lieutenant Colonel (later Colonel) John Fielding, Royal Signals, and the Property Services Agency project manager for the new airfield, set about establishing the conditions for digging, trenching and cable laying on Mount

Pleasant. When surveyed the area was found to be damp and not dissimilar to the geology found when cabling RAF Stanley; ie variable depth of soil and lots of rocks. Like Stanley, cables would in the main be directly buried and jointed in jointing pits that would most likely flood. Cable joints were to be made in heat-shrink materials that would withstand immersion in water for long periods of time.

The size of the airfield installation precluded the use of Army manpower and recourse had to be made to contract labour with Royal Signals acting in the role of "clerk of the works" and quality managers. As with the building of RAF Stanley, timing was critical. The planning work had to be completed in order that the MoD might complete their specifications for industry to compete for the work. A main contractor was to be chosen and made responsible for the complete installation (building the runway and buildings, installing cabling, electrical power, etc); a job eventually won by the consortium of Balfour-Kilpatrick.

Detailed cable planning was completed in the winter of 1984 following Ian's return to the UK and before he left CPA in March of that year to return to BT. On Ian's departure, the day-to-day responsibility for the cable network passed to Tom Hornby, and it was he who would oversee the installation that began later that year and was completed in August 1985.

San Carlos Water – scene of the Task Force landings on 21 May 1982

1983 TO 1991 –
MODERNISATION GATHERS PACE

The fall of the Berlin Wall on 9 November 1989 marked a dramatic end to the Cold War, and an end to Communist domination of Eastern Europe. Change and modernisation were in the air; six years earlier, the UK Post Office had transformed itself into a private telecommunications company called British Telecommunications plc (BT)

Introduction

The change in the status of Post Office Communications (POC) to a fully fledged private telecommunications company, British Telecommunications plc (BT) in 1983, brought about a fundamental change in the relationship between the Government and its principal communications supplier. Until that date, POC had supplied telecommunications services, personnel and products to all departments of Government. Included in these services were whole communications networks and the people required to operate and administer them. Charging was undertaken on the basis of the cost required to do the work, plus an agreed percentage of "profit" and very little work was placed with other suppliers by competitive tender.

The Government's drive to open up and regulate the telecommunications market in the UK required them to invite other telecommunications companies to bid for work that was previously the province of the POC.

The responsibility for the specification of the military's telecommunications needs rested with the Ministry of Defence's Procurement Executive and it was largely to this organisation that BT had to bid for new work. In turn in 1984 BT reorganised its sales force to provide a modern account management organisation that was better equipped and organised to deal with the commercial environment they now found themselves part of, which included competitive bidding.

BT Government National Accounts (re-titled BT Defence in 1999) was established in the same year to fulfil this function. Coincidental with the change in the status of BT, the Armed Forces began the first stages of their modernisation of the UK's military networks and it was on this work that both sides would learn the complexities of their new commercial relationship.

The Digitisation of the UK Service Networks

By the end of the Seventies the military networks of the Army, RAF and Royal Navy were beginning to show their age. The Falklands War underlined the need for strong lines of communication between the political leaders in the UK and the military authorities and commanders in the field. Between 1982, the year the Falklands War broke out and 1991, the year of the Gulf War, the MoD initiated a programme to modernise their military networks with digital stored programme controlled exchanges capable of carrying both speech and data. Each service produced a requirement for the design, installation and maintenance of individual and separate networks.

The Army Telephone Network (ATN) was replaced under the FASTNET programme, the RAF's under UNITER and the Navy's with the Naval Fixed Telecomms System (NFTS). All three were integrated speech and data networks, with some attempt in the early stages to provide interoperability through gateway nodes located at various points around the Country.

By 1978 the Army's manual network was creaking with age. Individual garrisons had separate manual switchboards for the connection of internal and incoming and outgoing calls. Garrisons were interconnected by private circuits operating antiquated signalling systems. The whole system was heavily dependent on manual switching which still relied on the intervention of several operators to make a call from, for example, Aldershot to Bicester, only a matter of 60 or 70 miles (96.5 or 112.7km) distant. During 1978 the network was automated with electro-mechanical private automatic branch exchanges (PABX) replacing the manual switchboards. With the aid of dialling codes soldiers were able to dial directly between garrisons using the private circuit network. Nevertheless, the speed of connections hardly rose above that of the manual network and the electro-mechanical switches were difficult to maintain even with a skilled workforce.

At the end of the Falklands conflict the task of modernising the ATN was addressed by issuing a series of specifications that would provide the military in the UK with a modern digital communications network. These specifications were "trawled" around the telephone exchange manufacturers and the licensed operators (BT and Mercury Communications Ltd) were brought together in an invitation to tender for Phase 1 of the FASTNET network. The specification called for a network capable of handling:

- high quality 64Kbit/s speech.

- high capacity digital exchanges modelled on private automatic branch exchange (PABX) traffic handling capacities and architectures.

- connection to the public telephone network by digital links running modern message based signalling protocols.

- connection between PABXs using digital private circuit signalling techniques.

- incoming calls with direct dialling-in that did not require the attention of an operator. This could not be done immediately.

- automatic calls within and between garrisons and where possible the other service networks.

BT was given responsibility for installing the first phase using the GEC Plessey Telecommunications (GPT) Integrated Services Digital PABX Exchange – the iSDX. Begining in June 1987 BT installed ninety-six switches at sixty-seven Army sites, with large transit switches being installed in each military district through which the dependent PABXs routed their calls. Phase 2 added a further fifty switches at thirty-five sites and Phase 3 yet more.

At about the same time as the Army were embarking on their FASTNET project, MoD(Air) was considering the feasibility of introducing an operational integrated digital network to support the air defence and support functions of Strike Command

THE INTEGRATED CIRCUIT★

Early in the transistor's development it became apparent that the base layer had to be kept thin in order to achieve an acceptable operating speed. A base of ten microns was needed for a frequency response of ten MHz. By 1955, the all-diffused silicon transistor had been produced by John Moll of Bell Labs. Based on diffusing the impurity atoms directly into a silicon wafer, this was a major step towards integrated circuit technology. An earlier transistor pioneer, William Shockley, left Bell Labs in the same year to set up Shockley Semiconductors at Palo Alto, California. Here he formed a team of young scientists and engineers to focus on silicon-based semi-conductors.

The US Government, concerned about the recent Russian success with Sputnik, provided large funds for research into the miniaturisation of electronic components. One company involved was Texas Instruments of Dallas, Texas, where work began under Jack Kilby. In July 1958, he first suggested the possibility of the extreme miniaturisation of a number of individual circuits and their components – resistors, capacitors, transistors and diodes – onto a single slice of silicon. By the end of August, he had produced a simplified circuit having the components interconnected with wire bonds. In January 1959, Robert Noyce of Fairchild Semiconductors had a similar idea. To improve the transistors being supplied to IBM, the company's Jean Hoerni had developed the planar process, which involved burying the active elements in a cocoon of silicon dioxide. Noyce took this a stage further, photo-etching the aluminium or gold conductors into the substrate. The initial batches were costly and relatively unreliable, but in 1960 Hoerni achieved a startling improvement in reliability by leaving the oxide diffusion layer mask in place. Six years later, J V Dalton completed the process by adding an overcoat of silicon nitride to provide a tough surface passivant and a seal against alkali ions. Since then, IC technology has continued growing and found its way into every facet of the electronics and related industries.

- Project UNITER. This network would provide secure speech and packet data facilities to link the UK radar sites and flying stations to the Command's headquarters and operations centre at High Wycombe in Buckinghamshire. Unlike FASTNET, UNITER was based on a variation of the European Signalling System No.7 which made the RAF network partially incompatible with those of the Army and Royal Navy.

Implementation of the UNITER network was awarded to GEC who deployed a network using their MX switch. Completed in 1988, the UNITER network supplied operational communications to some sixty RAF sites.

Like their colleagues in the Army and RAF, MoD(Navy) followed the same path and implemented an integrated voice and data network to support the naval establishments and dockyards around the UK. In scale this network was much smaller than FASTNET and UNITER, but was on a par in terms of its technical specification and performance. MoD(Navy) gathered their requirements under the title of NFTS and released an Invitation to Tender to industry in the late summer of 1986. BT was once again chosen to install their iSDX networks to meet the Navy's requirements and by 1989 the five node (20 switch) installation was completed.

Project BOXER

Having defined the three service networks, the MoD turned to the digital communications links that provided the vital arteries of the network. Throughout the decade the military had become more and more dependent on the civilian licensed operators to provide these links. Concerned that their wholesale dependence on these organisations and the costs they incurred might leave them vulnerable in time of war, the MoD set about proposing a military bearer network to protect their most valuable assets.

A tri-service project team was established at the Communications Projects Division in the School of Signals, Blandford, in 1980. The aim was to define the size and capacity of the new network, now allocated the codeword BOXER by the Ministry and to see whether the technology and costs would meet the MoD's requirements. It was proposed that much of this network would be a mixed civilian/military network, with the civil element being based on high capacity (for those days) 2 Mbit/s digital private circuits, backed-up by military owned digital links routed over a dedicated radio and fibre optic bearer network.

In proportion the Army had the largest share of the network, with the RAF coming a close second and the Royal Navy last. Detailed surveys of potential radio sites and feasibility studies into the fibre network showed the network would cost a great deal of money. The Army and Royal Navy were unable to bear these costs and they pulled out of the project in 1983, leaving the RAF to implement a slimmed down version of the design in support of UNITER. The scale of BOXER was too big for the RAF to implement on their own. The MoD(Air) overcame the problem by putting the whole project out to contract. BT were successful in being awarded the contract to implement the system and by the early 1990s had completed the installation and commissioned it to traffic.

Rationalisation and DFTS

There had been previous attempts but Project BOXER was the first serious attempt at providing a true national tri-service (purple) communications network. With the three services now in possession of some of the most modern military networks in the world, some means had to be found to integrate them into a true UK national military network. It was the Army that was to lead the way.

MoD Main Building

Having provided a country-wide integrated speech and data network, the MoD set about modernising its own communications, beginning with its headquarters in central London. The staff of the MoD were supported by an antiquated electromechanical PABX which was in need of replacement by a more modern digital system which supplied services and features in line with those of the three armed services. MoD Main, as it is generally known, had a unique traffic profile in as much as the majority of its calls, both incoming and outgoing, originated from the public civilian

network and therefore care had to be taken to avoid overloading the local exchanges to which it was to be connected. To overcome this problem BT proposed a hybrid solution based on a standard public exchange System X switch that was fully inter-connected to the public network, with four, later five, subordinate iSDXs serving 10,000 lines in the various departments of the Ministry. Digital links were provided to connect the incoming and outgoing public telephone subscriber network traffic to the System X and in those places where the traffic warranted it, inter-PBX System (DPNSS) links were introduced to carry those calls that were not destined to be connected to the public network.

BT's proposals were accepted and the exchanges were completed and the Ministry staff began transferring to their new network in 1989.

The RAF Telephone Network (RAFTN)

Alongside their main operational network, the RAF required a network protected to a lesser standard to support the administrative (admin) functions on UK stations (radar, flying and headquarters) and maintenance units. In 1992 MoD(Air) raised an Invitation to Tender for the project, but contracted the overall management to an external contractor (SERCO).

BT GNA bid for the switch element and was successful in being awarded a contract to supply ninety-six Nortel Meridian switches. These were installed between 1993 and 1995 to provide RAF stations with an integrated switch capable of supporting directly dialled incoming calls from the public network using an automated operator feature.

Nuclear bunkers and hardened shelters

By the late 1980s, Dave Spring was in charge of all the non UNITER work for the RAF at American and UK bases, working principally on the ASM Programme - the hardened Aircraft Shelters - funded mainly by NATO.   There were lighter moments as he remembers his time as Project Manager at RAF Wattisham where a lot of digging was needed to put in the required ducts:

> *"The BT man on site had agreed with the MoD that they could save time by digging a trench across the front of an aircraft hangar instead of going round three sides of it. The hangar contained a Tornado aircraft in for an overhaul, and their reasoning was that it would not be needed for at least some days. Unfortunately, unknown to them, the overhaul was finished and the plane was needed but it could not be removed because of the trench which lay neatly across the entrance to the hangar. The authorities were not best pleased."*

Vast amounts of money were being spent on developing and equipping nuclear bunkers for government and armed forces. Dave Spring's last assignment as a Project Manager before being promoted was to supervise the BT link for the bunker at High

Wycombe, now HQ for RAF Strike Command:

> *"The bunker is enormous. It is kept at an ambient temperature of 65 degrees but there are places where refrigerated air is pumped out and it is like working with a fridge door half open. Everything you touch is the same temperature. Most of the bunkers are like ships. They have tannoy systems which are used to give briefings. In the case of High Wycombe the system is audio visual with television screens at various sites in the bunker through which staff are told about the programme for the week."*

The Army Fixed Telecommunications Agency

At the end of 1989, two new agencies, ATTA, the Army Tactical Telecommunications Agency and AFTA, the Army Fixed Telecommunications Agency were established. They were to be the principal platforms from which future peacetime and war telecommunications systems would be launched. The principal aim of AFTA was to meet the Army's future needs for a fixed telecommunications service with particular emphasis on improving data communication.

Fixed communications had long since ceased to mean static. They had become one of the most exciting areas of modern telecommunication. Fixed communications started to embrace not only voice but also data networks, electronic mail, facsimile and video conferencing. Every form of telephone facility, including cellular systems, telepoint and voice messaging was included.

It was agreed that all of these needs should be met within a central or Defence Fixed Telecommunication Service. The initials DFTS were used for the first time. Before that could happen, however, a clear understanding and definition of what the Army needed had to emerge. Voice and data needs were unknown, let alone value added services. There was uncertainty about the role of the Royal Signals in all of this. Could it, given the present structure, plan, implement and manage an Army-wide fixed telecommunication network? There was a shortage of suitably trained manpower; nor was there in place an adequate system for measuring the effectiveness of current Army telecommunications services.

In 1989, DFTS plans were focused on the UK Theatre. The work of integrating the fixed telecommunication services of the three services would be conducted through the DFTS Planning and Implementation Team. They would also be responsible for worldwide fixed telecommunications for the three services and that would include the signal service known as Networks and Communications, a branch of the

MOD. Of its own initiative, this branch was developing a packet switched network which the DFTS Planning and Implementation Team was quick to adopt.

By 31 December 1989, the Army Fixed Telecommunications Agency had been established at Blandford with a number of targets:

- To define the Army's requirements for fixed telecommunications and value added services;

- to propose a revised Royal Signals organisation structure for fixed communications;

- to establish a strategy for the Army's fixed telecommunications for the 1990s;

- to address such matters as implementation plans, network management and the allocation of costs.

All of the above would need to be reviewed annually. Above all else, a team effort would be needed. Everyone concerned with fixed communications would be involved and would need to be committed.

These were the foundations on which subsequently the terms of the 1996 DFTS contract were finally agreed, although in the intervening seven years, new and almost revolutionary changes in defence planning and contracts had been introduced. A unique partnership between the Armed Services and INCA, an industrial consortium headed by British Telecom, was about to come into being.

But first, there was the Gulf War.

THE GULF WAR: UN PEACEKEEPING, BOSNIA AND KOSOVO

In February 1991, the largest armoured operation since World War Two was launched against Saddam Hussein from the desert Kingdom of Saudi Arabia. The objective was to liberate Kuwait, which had been illegally seized and occupied by Iraq on 9 August 1990.

Only six days later Eric Moore, one of BT Defence's Senior Systems Engineers, was invited to attend urgent talks at Rudloe Manor to discuss the RAF's likely communications requirements should the crisis lead to conflict. Rapid response times were vital. The first order received was for a BT MegaStream, the first of many, and a 48-hour delivery timescale was called for; normal delivery was 30 days. The RAF had their

General Rupert Smith at his HQ communications centre in the Gulf. British commanders of the 680,000 troops comprising 7 Armoured Brigade were able to telephone the UK from the desert via a satellite link. Supporting the troops on the ground and in the air were dedicated teams of BT personnel in the UK

requirement within 48 hours. This was a remarkable achievement, given the sophistication of a MegaStream's high capacity private services, which can be engineered at speeds of 2, 8, 34 or 140 Mbit/s.

The RAF's UNITER secure network programme also had to be accelerated. The main contract was with GPT, but BT provided the voice switching equipment based on the BTex product, together with the overall Network Management System. Between August and early December 1990, Eric Moore and his small London team were working at full stretch in a non-stop period of intense activity

Battlefield communications in the Gulf between forward troops and their commanders were supplied by the Royal Signals. This soldier on a reconnaissance patrol sends his information directly back to base so no opportunities for attack are lost

as Operation GRANBY took shape and the Coalition Forces built up in the Gulf.

On one occasion, 50 modems had to be delivered to RAF Brize Norton within hours. "We virtually robbed all of BT's stocks to meet the deadline", recalled Eric Moore, and despite a crisis when it was suddenly realised that no-one knew the correct voltage in Saudi Arabia, all difficulties were overcome and the requirement was achieved. Similar deadlines were constantly being set and agreed as a result of regular high-level liaison between the MoD and BT management; every single one was achieved.

The UNITER secure voice and data system was designed to provide the RAF's main UK communications infrastructure. In addition, they required a data network to support their overseas operations. BT met this need from their own product range, supplying Datelmux 7500 equipment based on Timeplex (LINK 2). The Datelmux

To ensure efficient communication between the UK MoD and the Gulf commanders, BT direct lines were put in place from the UK to the local Gulf PTO Satellite Ground Station and from there to military bases. Satellite Ground Stations were kept under close military guard at all times

(Dmux) is extremely complex; it comprises a highly sophisticated networking multiplexer which can be software configured from a control location. The central control of networks is a key factor in the design of digital voice and data networks, and DM 7500 control features enable diagnostics to be operated from one location, saving travelling time and enabling staff economies to be made.

Eric Moore and his team were helped to achieve their targets by being given the use of a workshop at RAF High Wycombe. By using BT and Cable & Wireless equipment, including satellites, it was possible to send the equipment both around the UK and out to aircraft operating bases in the Gulf area, including Cyprus, Bahrain, Incirluk and Riyadh. The RAF re-named the DM 7500 the ITDM – Independent Time Division Multiplex– network, and it went on to form part of the platform for the DFTS Point-to-Point Service (See Chapter Twelve).

From October 1990 onwards, the build-up of forces in the Gulf gathered momentum, and back in the UK during November and December, Eric Moore's work was extended to the Army, providing services and equipment for military ground satellite terminals at Colerne in Wiltshire. The communications requirement was growing so rapidly that commercial ground satellite terminals were also brought in.

Several months earlier, BT had been asked by the MoD to find a way for CNN news to be received directly in the UK Command nuclear blast-proof bunker at RAF High Wycombe through the CCTV system while maintaining the blast proof 'integrity' of the building – not an easy assignment. It was necessary, however, because the Commanders in the bunker found watching CNN news to be a good way of receiving intelligence and checking the progress of operations. Although Saddam Hussein must have known how useful this intelligence was to the Coalition Commanders, he was using the broadcasts for his own propaganda purposes and so allowed transmissions to continue throughout the conflict.

By the time of the Gulf deadline on 16 January 1991, Dave Spring was the BT Systems Engineer looking after the needs of the MoD. Eric Moore performed the same function for the RAF. They both helped to ensure that after the conflict no-one would be able to accuse BT of having delayed British objectives. Whatever circuits and services were needed got top priority; the paperwork followed. "Services" could range from setting up a video conferencing link in three days between Strike Command and Whitehall, to repairing Alan Clark's mobile phone. RAF aircraft took off from Brize Norton, the UK ground forces came principally from Germany and there were aircraft stationed at Incirluk in Turkey. The need for communications was urgent. Dave Spring remembers the sense of urgency at that time.

"Fixed communications in the Gulf itself were looked after by Royal Signals. We took over at the point where the satellite link reached the UK at RAF Oakhanger, and set up the fixed links with London, and from there set up circuits wherever they were needed. General (now Sir Peter) de la Billière was provided with a new secure telephone system called Patron, which allowed him to telephone the UK from his mobile unit in the desert via the satellite link to RAF Oakhanger – and thence to Whitehall, Brize Norton, Northwood or wherever. It was designed by the late Ken Bowden. Supporting the troops on the ground were a huge number of people back in the UK who arranged the logistics from their desks".

There was a particularly urgent need for point to point lines to be established linking the UK with Army and RAF units in the Gulf. These were new lines, set up from MoD establishments and Army and RAF locations, via BT Satellite Earth Stations. At the other end, in Saudi Arabia and the adjacent Gulf States, with the agreement of the corresponding Public Telecommunications Operators, new lines were extended to a port location, an air base, or a military Headquarters. There had to be full co-operation from the PTOs in each country to achieve what was needed and this had to be handled sensitively, taking Arab culture and customs into account. In the event, the co-operation from the Arab PTOs was remarkable, and things happened very quickly, sometimes overnight.

In basic terms, a BT direct line was put in place from the UK to the Satellite Ground Station operated by the local Gulf State PTO, and was then carried over normal telephone lines into military bases. The system worked so successfully that when the Gulf War was over, the additional facilities which had been set up in the UK were left in place for use should a similar situation occur again.

By February, when the air war was under way, the UNITER network was still being expanded. This required continuing BT involvement, and Eric Moore remembered "A lot of travelling around" from one end of the British Isles to the other. Qualified personnel always had to be on call, so BT staff at

When 7 Armoured Brigade were deployed to the Gulf from Germany in September 1990, they took with them the mobile Ptarmigan comunication system, shown here vehicle-mounted. Ptarmigan was a landmark in military communications, providing the link between tactical, satellite and land-based communications systems. The Gulf conflict was to be its first test in battle

155

the satellite stations and RAF High Wycombe worked round the clock.

In the Gulf conflict area no involvement of civilian personnel was allowed, so BT had to train RAF personnel in the use, servicing and maintenance of the equipment they had supplied.

Earlier, another aspect of BT involvement had begun as the 15 January ultimatum date approached. Eric Moore and his team were given deadlines for setting up additional communications facilities at RAF Lyneham to handle enquiries concerning possible casualties. A hospital at Chessington was chosen as the main base for the treatment and convalescence of returning wounded, and communications were also installed there. In the event the hospital was never needed and was later closed.

Eric Moore was involved as well in setting up a communications system enabling wives and families to keep in touch with troops in the Gulf. Much of the cost of this welfare operation was funded by BT, as it was to be later in Bosnia and Kosovo.

Britain's contribution to the multi-national Coalition Force of some 680,000 was 7 Armoured Brigade. This comprised two armoured regiments – Royal Scots Dragoon Guards and the Queens Royal Irish Hussars, one Infantry Battalion – 1 Bn Staffordshire Regiment – plus support units, totalling some 8,000 troops. The Royal Corps of Signals provided personnel for the Brigade Headquarters and detachments from 30 Signal Regiment supplied long distance communications back to London.

Soldiers of 30 Signal Corps making up the specialist TSEP – Technical System Executive and Plans – team did not reach the Gulf until December 1990, by which time Ptarmigan had been used for several months as a static communication system in several locations

COMMUNICATIONS SATELLITES

Artificial orbiting satellites were conceived by science fiction author Arthur C Clarke in 1945. But they remained fiction until the mid-1950s, due to a lack of sufficiently powerful launch rockets. Improvements made in ballistic missile technology then provided the answer, and on 4 October 1957 the Russians launched the first satellite, Sputnik One.

On 31 January the following year, the United States launched their own satellite, Explorer 1, on board a Juno 1 missile. These successes suggested the use of satellites for long-distance communications. The first live two-way telephone call by satellite was made in August 1960 via Echo 1, a metallised plastic balloon which reflected radio waves. Next came the first true artificial telecommunications relay satellite, Telstar, launched on 10 July 1962. It could receive and transmit signals between fast tracking antennas at Andover, Maine, in the US, Goonhilly in England and Pleumeur-Bodou in France.

These early versions were low earth orbiting satellites, which had to be accurately tracked. Later came geostationary orbit satellites – also foreseen by Arthur C Clarke in 1945 – which orbited at a height of 22,370 miles/36,000km directly above the equator. They completed an orbit at the same rate as the earth's rotation, and covered a larger area with their signals. The Syncom satellites, developed by the Hughes Aircraft Company, successfully achieved geostationary earth orbit – GEO – in August 1964, doing away with the need for expensive and complex fast-tracking antennas; they remain first choice for communications satellites.

In 1961 US President Kennedy proposed a worldwide satellite network. Three years later the International Satellite Organisation Intelsat was formed. Their first product, Earlybird, achieved GEO orbit above the Atlantic on 6 April 1965. It provided 240 telephone channels, or one television channel, with good telephone communications both ways across the Atlantic. By the end of 1969 two more Intelsats over the Pacific and Indian Oceans were in position, giving global coverage.

Today, the growth of land mobile – cellular – communications has resulted in the re-use of low earth orbit LEO satellites to support private centre networks. The first of these, the Iridium constellation, completed half their network at the end of 1998. Their chief use is in video broadcasting, and in global telephony they are still used for immediacy, especially where the infrastructure does not reach the undersea fibre optic cables.

PTARMIGAN

When the Gulf crisis broke, 7 Armoured Brigade were in Germany. They deployed to the Gulf in September 1990, taking with them the Ptarmigan communication system which was to be tested for the first time in battle. Because it was a landmark in military communications, providing the bridge between tactical, satellite and land-based communications systems, it merits inclusion in any account of communications during the Gulf War.

Lieutenant Colonel Peter Barron of 30 Signal Regiment, then Captain, was attached to 1 BR Corps and based at Bielefeld in Germany. He takes up the story:

"Planning began as soon as the commitment had been made to send 7 Armoured Brigade. Although the troops left for the Gulf in September, there was no one from the Corps with them and when we were finally ordered to the Gulf in early December 1990, we had already had two false starts. I was to go as Frequency Manager, which was my job with 1 BR Corps at the time. I was told that I could take a team of three – far fewer than when we exercised normally. The team was called TSEP, which stood for Technical System Executive and Plans. We were to carry out frequency management for the Ptarmigan system which was to dominate tactical communication during the whole of the Gulf Conflict".

While Ptarmigan was being used initially as a static system it had to be well camouflaged against missile attack, as shown above. The problem of obtaining accurate frequency assignments, made more difficult by dust, heat and climatic conditions, was solved by the rapid deployment of new Frequency Assignment Management Equipment – FAME – which was still under trial

By the time the TSEP team arrived in December 1990, Ptarmigan had been on the ground for several months and was being used as a static communication system in a number of locations. There were a number of problems to solve. No terrain database of the Gulf area existed, so there were no mapping co-ordinates on which to make frequency assignments. The Frequency Assignment tool which was currently being used by 1 (BR) Corps was very old and could not cope with the dust and heat and climatic conditions. A new Frequency Assignment Management Equipment – FAME – still under trial, was therefore rapidly deployed.

Exercising and planning had been going on since September and from early January 1991, the Brigade began to move forward. By the end of the month Scud attacks had become frequent events and the TSEP team spent a number of nights on watch and wearing respirators.

Ptarmigan performed well and provided vital communications. The terrain was largely flat, although interrupted in places by sand dunes and rocky outcrops. The system, therefore, did not need to be highly mobile and at one stage Ptarmigan maintained communications in an unbroken chain for 540km, longer than had ever been achieved before. The system was built for survival and every network included several loops. As the troops dispersed over the vast desert terrain, the network become ever more stretched until it was fairly fragile.

There were two principal problems. As the system became extended, there were problems with the single channel radio access system which provided the vital link between the front line troops and the trunk system which fed into the rear satellite link back to the UK. The establishment of this satellite link caused problems as well because after arrival in the Gulf, the Ptarmigan database had to be rebuilt using certain records. Back in Britain, those establishing the satellite link were replicating these records, which had to be done in isolation. The fear was that when the two were put together they would conflict, but this proved groundless.

The war was the first operational deployment of the Ptarmigan Communications System in a Battle Zone. The ripples from the aftermath of the Gulf War had hardly begun to disappear before another and much more prolonged source of conflict arose in the Balkans. Once again BT were called upon to provide communications support as and where needed. The RAF's UNITER network was fully functional by this time and equipment which had been used in the Gulf was redeployed to Italy and to Incirluk in Turkey, from where the "No Fly" zones were being administered.

Some BT equipment is still being used by NATO in Bosnia. This situation is not without problems as many of the systems there were not designed to be compatible.

The map shows the locations of the various republics into which the Former Yugoslavia fragmented follow-ing the death of Marshal Tito in 1980 and the subsequent end of the Cold War. Kosovo is not marked because it is officially a province of Serbia, not an independent state, but it is shown here as the northern part of Albania

Bosnia and Kosovo

Introduction

Since 1945, the British Army have taken part in many UN and NATO Forces peacekeeping and humanitarian operations. All were different, but none more bitter than the conflicts in Bosnia in 1992-95 and Kosovo in 1999.

Over the last decade, the former Republic of Yugoslavia has been painfully torn apart. As this book goes to press there are still areas of conflict in spite of UN Security Council Resolutions, peacekeeping missions and the armed air intervention by NATO in 1999.

The current fragmentation began with the death of Marshal Tito in 1981, but the area has always been at odds with itself despite the post-World War One name of the Kingdom of the Serbs, Croats and Slovenes. The name was changed to Yugoslavia in 1929 in an attempt to encourage a national identity.

In 1941 the Germans overran the country, and Yugoslavia was partitioned. Most of the recent bitterness between Serbs, Croats and Slovenes stems from the Croat and Slovene support for Hitler during World War Two. Following the defeat of the Nazi-backed Croat regime by Tito and his communist partisans, Bosnia-Herzegovina became one of six Yugoslav republics, organised along Soviet lines, but after Tito's death it became increasingly difficult to preserve any unity.

At the beginning of the 1990s, as the former Warsaw Pact countries renounced communism and embraced Western democracy, the republics making up Yugoslavia made their dash for independence.

The Serb majority had always been the dominant power in Yugoslavia, and the problems began in 1991 when Slovenia declared itself independent. In the middle of the same year, Croatia followed suit. The Serb army moved in to protect Serbs living in Croatia. A vicious civil war followed as the Serbs fought for their own homeland and declared a Serbian Republic of Krajina inside Croatia.

Much worse was to follow as Bosnia-Herzegovina seceded from Yugoslavia later in the year. Civil war broke out as Bosnian Serbs and Croats alike made a land grab for as much territory as possible from the Bosnian Muslims, targeting them for attack and later persecution.

In early 1992, a ceasefire was negotiated to halt the civil war between the Croats and Serbs in Croatia. The UN sent a peacekeeping force – UNPROFOR – to protect and demilitarise four UN Protected Areas; around 14,000 personnel were initially involved.

SATELLITE COMMUNICATION

A Tactical Satellite Ground station is usually housed in a vehicle or a container. Speech, data and fax are transmitted upwards to a Skynet satellite and down into the satellite hubs in the UK at Defford, Oakhanger and Colerne. At the satellite hubs, communication signals are interfaced onto the BT or other system provider and sent to the MoD and other Headquarters in the UK by digital lines. Signals are routed back along the same route.

Refugees, seen here protected by British UN soldiers, were assisted in communicating with their relatives in other parts of Europe by BT, who provided two mobile containers equipped with ten telephones. Subsequently the containers were made available to British, Dutch and Belgian troops to make welfare calls home

Operation GRAPPLE

The British ground troops sent to Bosnia at the end of 1992 at the UN's request were part of an extended UN Protection Force. The aim was to escort aid convoys into war-ravaged areas. The 1 Cheshire Regiment was deployed, and integrated into the UN Chain of Command. The British were allocated the central region of Bosnia where the fighting was heaviest. Bases were established at Split, Tomislavgrad, Gornji Vakuf and Vitez.

As had been the case in Croatia, the Dutch provided all UN communications within Bosnia, but not facilities for national contingents to communicate with their home Headquarters nor within their own Battalions. Unlike Croatia, the Bosnian civil

While the Dutch provided all UN communications in Bosnia, individual national contingents had to provide their own, both with their home HQ and their Battalions. Neither Ptarmigan nor wide area VHF radio were sufficiently effective, and Transportable Satellite Ground Terminals were used by the Royal Signals, as shown above

telecommunications system was either unreliable or non-existent.

The UK therefore had to establish their own reliable high grade communications. The nature of the terrain meant that Ptarmigan or a wide area VHF radio network could not be used with the same ease as in the desert.

Transportable Satellite Ground Terminals were needed to carry the Data circuits which linked the UN Headquarters in Split, the troops on the ground and the MoD and HQ UKLF in the UK. In the field, High Frequency radio remained the main tactical communications system.

In March 1993, NATO declared a No-Fly Zone over Bosnia, enforced by the deployment of NATO aircraft to Italy. From the outset the RAF were involved. In May 1993, a British Air HQ was established at UN BHC HQ in Kiseljak to support the No-Fly Zone. A tactical satellite ground terminal was deployed and provided communications between Kiseljak and the RAF in Italy, HQs in the UK and COMBRIT-FOR in Split.

In 1994 Lieutenant General Sir Michael Rose took over as commander of UN Forces in Bosnia and the main British HQ moved from Kiseljak to Sarajevo. During 1994, satellite ground terminals continued to provide national communications for General Rose and his staff.

BT and the Welfare Station

BT were responsible throughout UN operations for providing the connectivity for all satellite communication at the UK end. The soldiers on the ground also had particular reason to be grateful to BT. For Christmas 1992, the latter offered servicemen a special free facility enabling them to make contact with their families – an offer gratefully accepted by the UK MoD.

The mission was not an easy one. Because of the widespread devastation, no telephone infrastructure existed capable of providing access to International Direct Dialling. The only practical option was via a satellite, and early in December 1992 BT flew a Welfare Telephone System from the UK to Split.

Only one system was available, and as at that time the Cheshire Regiment – the largest number of British troops in Bosnia – were deployed at Vitez, it became the chosen site. Being a high-security area, civilian technicians could not operate and service the terminal and telephones. Instead, a military technician from 30 Signal Regiment attended a short BT training course on how to assemble and operate the station.

He flew back to Bosnia with this, and on arrival in Split he and his fellow-signallers loaded the equipment onto several military lorries for the journey to Vitez. Because of severe weather, hold-ups at checkpoints, and fighting in areas through which the convoy had to pass, the short journey eventually took over 24 hours.

Having finally reached Vitez, they set to work assembling the station. Despite a lack of accompanying instructions, bad weather and battle conditions, the satellite dish was safely mounted on top of a building and the Welfare Station was operational.

There were ten telephones, providing ten lines of video and speech 24 hours a day, with calls limited to ten minutes. Timing was ensured by issuing the troops with ten-minute phone cards. Before this, welfare calls were only available using the three military speech circuits from the satellite ground station. Their quality was poor, and they could only be used for a few hours at night when they were not needed for operational use. Calls were presented in London and from there on BT lines to the UK and Germany, all charged at local rates.

The new BT Welfare Station opened in good time for Christmas. The first video call from a soldier in Vitez to his family in Fallingbostal in Germany received much media coverage. However the video link was withdrawn almost immediately, because it was expensive in terms of bandwidth and the main need was for speech lines. Around 1,400 calls were made every day, all paid for by BT.

For Christmas 1993, with more planning time available, BT widened their welfare offer. Although the BT International Operator Services had worked well, adding an understanding human element in handling calls direct from military bases, the future was seen by BT as lying with direct dialling. By December 1993 this, together with video links, had been extended to the UK, Cyprus, Germany, Gibraltar and the Irish Republic. From 4 January 1994 Cardphones were used, for which cards were available from NAAFI outlets. They were also capable of taking cards sent to the troops as presents from the UK.

The success of this operation was due to exceptionally good satellite coverage and the co-operation of the Bosnian PTT in understanding that the facilities were solely intended for the welfare of UN peacekeeping troops.

In December 1995, UN activities in Bosnia ended and NATO took over. The whole operation became more robust and changed from a peace-keeping to a peace-enforcement role. But the story told here, of BT's contribution to Britain's UN peacekeeping forces, is one of professionalism and dedication in hostile, dangerous and inhospitable conditions.

Throughout the Kosovo crisis BT's Video and Broadcasting Services, with their TES fleet, helped the MoD to give excellent and authentic media briefings

Kosovo

Operation AGRICOLA

As many feared, the terrible ethnic conflict which had torn Bosnia apart spilled over into Kosovo at the beginning of 1999. BT's Eric Moore was again involved. Only eight years separated the Gulf War from Operation AGRICOLA in Kosovo, but during that time there had been a communications revolution. Demands for ever more sophisticated information and data had become difficult to meet. In particular, BT found that satellite users were demanding greater bandwidths in order to handle all the information traffic. A civilian parallel would be between the narrow country roads which were originally adequate to handle the limited amount of motor traffic in the 1930s compared to the six lane highways required today.

BT's answer to this demand for increased bandwidths – which have expanded eightfold From 64 Kbit/s to 512 Kbit/s – was to put additional MegaStreams and more fibre optic cable into a number of the sites.

The campaign of air strikes against Serbia during April and May 1999 was a direct result of NATO intervention to prevent President Slobodan Milosevic's attempted ethnic cleansing of Kosovo. It was portrayed to the world through a multi-media campaign which even made use of the Internet. This media campaign was waged using public briefings by leading statesmen in Washington, London and Brussels.

The UK MoD's Defence Crisis Management Organisation presented the daily press media briefings in London. These were considered to be the best because of their broad scope, but there was a desire to improve them still further. The Organisation happened to be working with BT Defence and asked if they were in a position to provide broadcast quality satellite facilities from the Balkans which could be fed direct into the daily 11.30 to midday press briefings held in the MoD Main Building's South Concourse.

BT had vehicle mounted Transportable Earth Stations – TESs – in both Montenegro and Albania, constantly moving around to cover both the plight of the refugees and the build-up of NATO support troops. These TESs were also stationed in the UK, making them ideal for handling the requested transmissions.

How BT helped the refugees and the peacekeepers

BT assisted Kosovar Albanian refugees by providing two containers equipped

BT's Transportable Earth Station was based in front of the MoD's South Concourse throughout the Kosovo crisis, providing 5/10 satellite transmissions from the Balkans for the daily press briefings

with ten telephones at sites known as Kukes 1 and Kukes 2, from where they could dial their relatives in other parts of Europe. This process was also helped by the setting up of a BT call centre in Munich, staffed by Kosovar Albanians, which acted as a control point to help reunite families which had become separated.

One of the containers in Albania was later moved up to Pristina, where it was used by British troops to make welfare calls home. The other was made available to Dutch and German Troops in Prizren for free welfare calls. They good-heartedly charged themselves for these calls, and used the money to purchase materials for their off-duty work refurbishing kitchens in hospitals and schools.

They were also able to fund the production of a booklet for schoolchildren stressing the importance of mine awareness, as the schools had been used as barracks by Serb troops and were in a dangerous state.

The containers were finally switched off at the end of September 1999.

Together BT and the MoD established a procedure in which the latter would brief BT Video Broadcasting Services – VBS – on what was required, and a TES, together with a CBS camera crew working with BT to provide television coverage to the US, would be sent to meet whoever was due to be interviewed.

At the same time in the UK, another TES in the MoD's south car park would receive the video and audio. These were then taken in onto the MoD's Audio-Visual mixing desk, and by satellite across London by the BBC for onward transmission within the UK and abroad.

This additional live material was brought in by BT for half-hour sessions on over 20 occasions during the crisis. These sessions often involved UK Ministers discussing the situation with British commanders in the field, and on one occasion with the Albanian Foreign Secretary, before journalists were invited to question a guest expert appearing on large-screen TV.

The coverage provided by BT on occasion extended even further. Some sessions involved their linking the UK MoD with Washington or Brussels, so BT's worldwide facilities were able to create a series of global briefing sessions.

Another notable occasion masterminded by BT during the build-up of support troops in Albania was transmitting live television pictures from a Transportable Earth Station in the capital, Tirana, showing the arrival of the US Apache Attack Helicopters.

Throughout the Kosovo crisis, BT's Video and Broadcasting Services, with their TES fleet, proved an international asset and helped the UK MoD to establish the acknowledged excellence and on-the-spot authenticity of their media briefings.

The end of the NATO air campaign, however, was not the end of the BT story in Kosovo. Peacekeeping troops remained, and so did the problems. The majority of Serbs departed, and many Kosovar Albanians returned. When the Serbs left, they took with them as much useful material as they could transport. Particularly hard-hit was the local telephone company, PTK. This had been staffed mainly by Kosovar Albanian engineers, with Serb managers. The latter had joined the Serb exodus, driving away in the PTK trucks and taking with them all the company's toolkits.

BT came to the rescue, with the help of 19 Mechanised Brigade at Catterick, by sending out to Pristina 15 complete toolkits and a quantity of engineers' cold-weather clothing, which had also disappeared with the departing Serbs.

THE DEFENCE FIXED
TELECOMMUNICATIONS SYSTEM

The digital age has revolutionised all aspects of military communication. Among the landmarks were BT's contracts for the design and installation of fixed communications systems for all three armed services. FASTNET was developed for the Army, NFTS for the Royal Navy and the Air Force had its UNITER (not supplied by BT) and BOXER Networks. In addition, BT designed and installed a comprehensive voice and data communications system in the MoD Whitehall complex.

The contract for the Defence Fixed Telecommunications System was awarded to INCA by the UK Ministry of Defence and signed on 25 July 1996

By the mid 1990s, the fixed telecommunications systems being operated by UK armed forces consisted of many separate, overlapping and inter-connected networks. Most had evolved independently of each other during the years since first the GPO and then BT and others had responded to the Forces' needs.

Many of these systems and networks had become costly to maintain and functions were wastefully duplicated. Some needed to be replaced. Others needed to be modernised. A feasibility study initiated in 1987 (see Chapter 10) resulted eight years later in the Ministry of Defence inviting tenders for the provision of a new Defence Fixed Telecommunications System (DFTS) which would meet all their communications requirements until 2010. A single fixed telecommunications system had

169

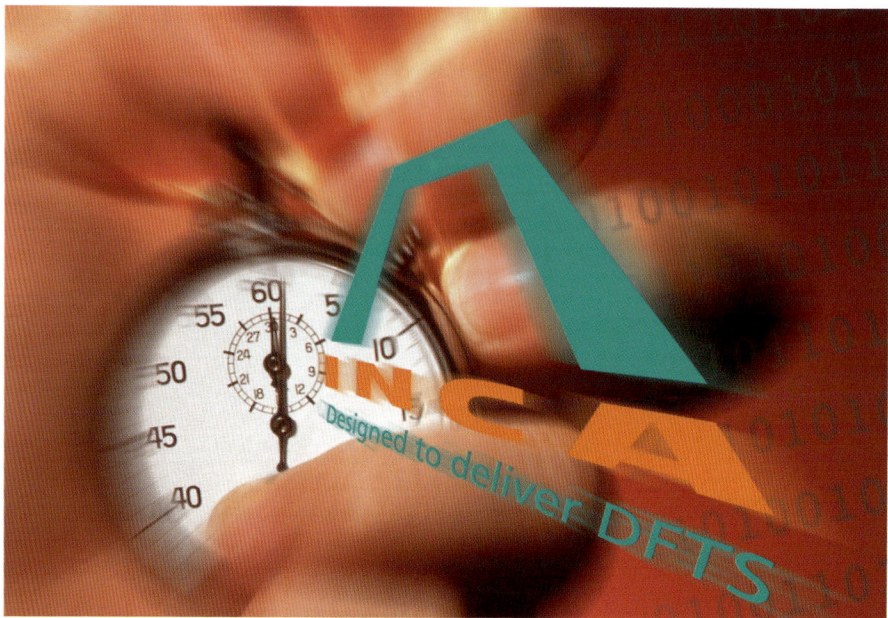

been identified as the keystone of the strategy.

The project began as a conventional public sector procurement of assets, but became a pathfinder PFI project. The final stage of the competition was between teams led by BT and RACAL.

The contract was officially signed on 25 July 1996 between the Ministry of Defence and BT, under the government's Private Finance Initiative (PFI). The BT team was named INCA. It was significant in the history of military telecommunication not least because ownership of Britain's fixed military communication networks was being handed over to a commercial organisation. The MoD were promised savings of around £100mn over the ten years of the contract through the rationalisation of defence telecommunications, then provided by the three services and MoD Centre, into a single operation.

What is INCA?

The INCA consortium combines the technical expertise of BT, the project management skills of Lockheed Martin, the security know-how of GEC Marconi and the experience of GPT Strategic Communications (since the contract was signed

The figure shows the 46 previous services which are now part of the Defence Fixed Telecommunications System

9 Point-to-Point Data
7 Circuit Switched Voice
5 Point-to-Point Voice
2 Packed Switched Data
1 Circuit Switched Data

3 Circuit Switched Voice
1 Point-to-Point Data
1 Circuit Switched Data

MOD Centre

Army

Defence Fixed Telecommunications System

Navy

RAF

3 Circuit Switched Voice
1 Circuit Switched Data
1 Packed Switched Data
1 Point-to-Point Voice
1 Point-to-Point Data

2 Circuit Switched Voice
3 UNITER Circuit Switched Voice
2 UNITER Circuit Switched Data
1 UNITER Packed Switched Data
1 UNITER special
1 BOXER Point-to-Point Data

The previous services now included in the Defence Fixed Telecommunications System (DFTS)

GEC Marconi and GPT have merged). Until the year 2007, INCA, as DFTS' prime contractor, will provide all the capital investment needed to deliver the fixed telecommunication services which Britain's armed services need. INCA will respond to changing system and service requirements just as BT continually respond to the needs of customers in the civilian sector. Every aspect of DFTS is INCA's responsibility, including any risk factors. The Headquarters for the project is based at Basil Hill Barracks in Corsham, Wiltshire where INCA and MoD staff work side by side.

The concept of the provision of service for communications as opposed to asset purchase was a new one for the MoD. It meant that MoD need no longer concern itself with the nuts and bolts of technology and wires but focus much more on what their users and customers actually require. It was now INCA's responsibility to provide the services that met the requirement.

To achieve success, a joint approach was vital; trust and co-operation were integral to the project's success. A partnership needed to be developed between the armed services and INCA, which was about to take on roles and responsibilities that were previously carried out by the MoD. During the early days of the contract, this fundamental change in attitude was one of the most difficult aspects to achieve.

DFTS had as its mission the provision within the UK of a single fixed telecommunications service which was secure, cost-effective and capable of expansion. INCA were to take into their ownership all existing systems – 46 different networks provided by four separate organisations – and would integrate, rationalise and reform them into six new services, upgrading, modernising or replacing the equipment in the process. It would be managed by one organisation, the Defence Communications Services Agency (DCSA), established in April 1998 and officially launched on 16 July the same year. On 1 April 2000 the DCSA became part of the Defence Logistics Organisation – DLO.

One major benefit of DFTS is the availability of management information for the MoD for the first time. Costs can be analysed and advice obtained on the most efficient and economical use of the telephone and data handling systems. This is of major importance given the technological explosion of the late 1990s.

The beginning

On New Year's Day 1998, Huw Rees, Programme Director, and his team of ten walked into an empty office floor of the BT building at North Star House, Swindon. During the following twelve months, those ten people swelled to nearly 200. Around

130 people work from BT's North Star House in Swindon with about 60 in Reading and about 20-30 at Corsham. A LAN links the three locations enabling any staff member in any location to go to the nearest terminal and access any accumulated mail. DCSA staff involved in the project also have access to the same LAN. This assists with the forging of the partnership.

One of the biggest challenges facing Huw Rees and INCA was to establish the vital element of trust between the contractor and the MoD. MoD staff have traditionally tended to regard contractors in procurement contracts with something akin to suspicion. In this case the development of a partnership and a joint approach was fundamental to the project being able to meet all the target dates which were agreed.

One of the biggest challenges facing Huw Rees, Programme Director, and his team at INCA was to establish the vital element of trust between the contractor and the MoD. As he said later, "We are developing a partnership . . . this is a fundamental change"

There was of course the challenge of persuading the service chiefs that the ownership of the entire military fixed communications system was safe in INCA's hands. Historically the services had done most things in the communications world their own way. Now a third party – and from the private sector – was on the scene and this would require a new approach.

As Huw Rees put it a year into the contract, "We are developing a partnership. We at INCA are taking on the role and responsibilities of the MoD in this particular area and this is a fundamental change". In some areas responsibility is shared. But mainly the objective is that the armed services specify what they want and INCA provides it. That was and is a cultural change and much energy was channelled into developing the crucial understanding on both sides of how the partnership would work in practice.

There was also the need to get over the crucial message that while charges might initially seem high, they covered a comprehensive and guaranteed service which avoided the need for a whole range of overhead and manpower costs which traditionally fell to the MoD to pay. There is no equipment maintenance, no depreciation, no cost of updating or replacement, no need to have a spares department, and no need to train and pay service engineers, telephone operators or run a Directory Enquiry Service. All of this is included in the price of a service. Reduced to basic terms, it could be compared to renting a TV/Video package with a service guarantee, rather than buying the equipment and then having to pay if anything goes wrong or if the equipment needs replacing or upgrading.

INCA also takes the risks involved in developing new services. They have to make sure that the service they provide is up to the job. If they introduce a service which has a low pick up rate, they bear the loss. On the other hand, if a new service proves popular, INCA – as well as the forces – are the winners. INCA publish a catalogue listing the whole range of services now available, from which authorised

telecommunication officers (ATOs) select and pay for what they need. Through the Helpdesk, INCA give as much advice and guidance as the ATOs need.

Prices now vary, depending on what is being provided, of what grade, how robust, how sophisticated, how resilient and what level of guaranteed service is required. INCA can advise on the level of service needed to do a specific job. This means that if a less sophisticated system or type of service is good enough for the job, this is what is suggested and, if agreed, provided and charged for. A "Rolls-Royce" 100 per cent guaranteed service inevitably costs more..

Transition and Migration

There were two principal initial stages to the contract – Transition (August 1997 to June 1998) and Migration (June 1998 – May 2000). At the beginning of the tran-

FIBRE OPTIC COMMUNICATIONS

The fact that light will travel down a transparent medium has been known since 1854, when John Tyndall demonstrated it to the Royal Society. Using water as the medium, he also proved that light would bend when the water curved. This property of light was later adapted for lighting systems and surgical applications.

In the 1920s, John Logie Baird and the American Clarence W Hansell patented the idea of using glass rods to transmit television and fax images. Modern fibre optics began in 1930, when Heinrich Lamm, a German medical student, first assembled a bundle of optical fibres to carry an image. These were made from single strands of glass, gathered into bundles, and had light transmitted through them.

Although the experiment worked, considerable amounts of light escaped from each fibre and interfered with the others. Further research was needed. In 1954, the Dutch scientist Abraham Van Heel tried coating his fibres in an outer layer of glass having a lower refractive index. This protected the core fibre from distortion, and greatly reduced both interference between fibres and light loss. By 1960, glass clad fibres with an attenuation of 1dB per metre were being manufactured – adequate for surgery but not for telecommunications.

Two years earlier, Alec Reeves of Standard Telecommunications Laboratories – STL – suggested using frequencies operating in the optical domain as a possible way to achieve greater telephone transmission bandwidth. The use of optical fibres was considered, because their performance was similar to the plastic dielectric waveguides then used in microwave systems. A small team at STL, led by Antoni Karbowiak – who had earlier worked for Reeves – and assisted by Charles Kao, established that the high attenuation of fibres was due to the high level of impurities introduced into the silica glass. In December 1964 Karbowiak was succeeded by Kao as the manager of optical communications.

Kao continued his work, this time in association with George Hockham, also of STL. They calculated that if fibre loss could be reduced below 20 dB per km, then fibres having an equivalent transmission capacity to 200 TV channels, or 200,000 telephone circuits, were feasible. Their findings, published in the July 1966 Proceedings of the Institution of Electrical Engineers – IEE – were read by Frank Roberts, a staff engineer at the Post Office Research Laboratory, Dollis Hill. He saw the potential of optical fibres, and persuaded his deputy director Jack Tillman and others to invest £12mn to study ways of reducing their loss.

When the INCA contract was signed, the armed forces had between them 46 different networks, some duplicating each other. Rationalisation was an immediate need, and the first phase of the DFTS Network Management Control Centre (NMCC) at Corsham, shown above, went live on 15 December 1997

sition stage a full survey was carried out at over 400 MoD sites. The objective was to list and assess all the existing equipment which INCA would take into their ownership. Bit by bit INCA took over all the then existing telecommunications networks and managed them. At the time the contract was signed there were 46 of these net-

The takeover of the RAF BOXER and UNITER networks took place between January and September 1998, although for security reasons they remained owned by the MoD. Here Chief Petty Officer Tony Blackburn, RN – right – accepts the system password from Corporal Neil Parker, RAF, at the handover ceremony

works and in Huw Rees's words "We put our arms around these 46 systems, pulled them together and ran them".

Many of the systems duplicated each other. For example, each of the three services had their own telephone system. They were linked up through "Gateways", but the gateways did not allow an adequate and fully integrated service.

The first phase of the DFTS Network Management Control Centre (NMCC) went live at Corsham at one minute past midnight on 15 December 1997.

The Transfer of assets from MoD to INCA (Transition) began at the same time. The Defence Packet Switch Network, now known as PSS, was the first ever transfer of an MoD communications asset to a private sector company. It was followed by the takeover between January and September 1998 of the RAF BOXER and UNITER Networks. These two networks, providing telecommunications resistant to nuclear attack, were the only exception to the rule that INCA would take full ownership of all existing assets. They remained in MoD ownership while INCA accepted full responsibility for guaranteed performance, availability, maintenance and network management. Handover of all voice networks was completed on 22 June 1998.

As each network was transferred from the MoD to INCA, areas of operation and procedures (network control, Helpdesk, billing, design and performance management) were brought together under one single control.

The six DFTS services

The main voice or telephone service is called **The Circuit Switched**

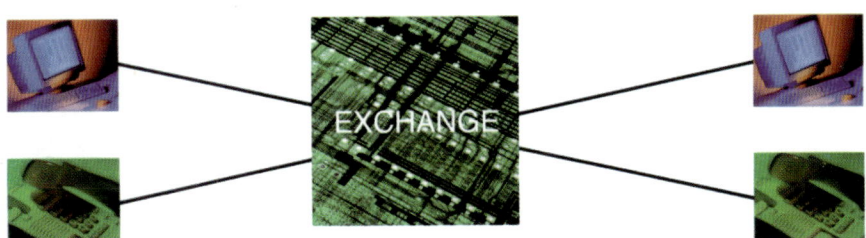

Services 4 and 5: Circuit Switched Voice and Data
No permanent connections exist between terminals, but a digital circuit is established by a switching centre in an exchange when a transmission is made. This remains as a dedicated connection for the duration of the transmission. Once the transmission ends, the circuit is terminated

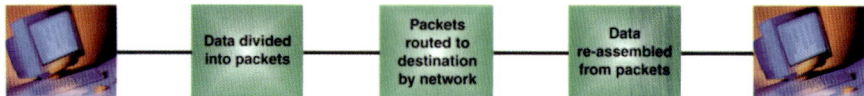

Service 3: Packet Switched Data

Digital data transmissions are divided into groups of data or 'packets' to allow them to share the network with other transmissions. Packets are re-assembled at receiving terminal to form original transmission. Allows more efficient use of network

(Telephone) Service. In June 1998, the RAF's telephone network was the first to be upgraded and connected to BT's Core FeatureNet telecommunications infrastructure. The Core FeatureNet was designed principally to handle public voice communications and is part of BT's UK Telephone Service which includes over 6,000 modern System X exchanges. Built-in intelligence automatically routes DFTS calls over the network. The Core FeatureNet is a virtual "ring-fenced" private network which prevents non-MoD users from getting into it. It also provides guaranteed bandwidth to ensure that MoD calls are never hampered or restrained during periods of heavy use by other BT subscribers.

One of the first benefits of DFTS was the introduction of a **new numbering system.** Instead of the long dialling codes which were used between the different branches of the UK's Armed Services, each site now has its own four-digit site location number, followed by an extension. This new code structure simplifies telephone numbering and offers better and quicker access to connections between networks.

There are two major data services. First the **Packet Switched Service**. The Packet Switched Service now provides the defence community including the British Forces in Germany with an improved single unified data network. Using the DFTS trouble shooting software, Clarify, any system failures on the different elements which make up the Packet Switched Service can be recorded and tracked.

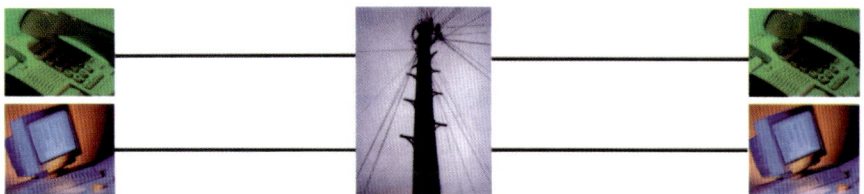

Services 1 and 2: Point-to-Point Voice and Data

All connections between terminals are by permanent lines

In the Millennium year the BT-led INCA team received the accreditation for IGS from the Communications-Electronics Security Group (CESG), the Government's Centre of Excellence for Information Security. Team members shown – from left to right – are: John Hogan, INCA Evaluation Manager; Dave Byron, Director, Marconi Secure Systems; Huw Rees, Programme Director, INCA; Dr Richard Walton, Director, Communications, Electronic Security Group; Dave Edwards, Design & Implementation Manager, INCA; John Ducey, Channel Director, Government Sales, Nortel; and Jo Alwyn, INCA Security Manager

The second and the most important data service is known as the **Local Area Network (LAN) Interconnect Service**. Launched in February 1998, this new service enables the defence community to share and exchange computerised information at exceptionally high speeds; they can do this either on an "any to any" basis or as part of a closed user group. LAN Interconnect enabled the MoD to create a secure Intranet environment where facilities like Web browsers, e-mail, Web Services and other Internet applications could be developed and adapted for MoD users.

The LAN Interconnect Service is available at both RESTRICTED (RLI) and SECRET (SLI) levels. The service is also available to closed user groups. In March 2000, MoD users who were connected to the RESTRICTED LAN Interconnect (RLI) Service were offered the ability to make full use of the Internet through the introduction of a secure electronic communication service previously not available to them. This is BT's Internet Gateway Service (IGS). For the first time, the MoD could gain access to the World Wide Web and other information resources secure in the knowledge that the necessary built-in system safeguards and protection mechanisms were firmly in place. This is a giant leap forward. The IGS allows the MoD to com-

Setting up the DFTS involved creating a new numbering system, so an MoD Centralised Operator Service was established at four principal Centres – Dumbarton, Kettering, Wakefield and St Helens, shown here. They offer a single point of contact for all internal and external enquiries, and incorporate a new Directory Enquiries Service established in May 1998

municate with commercial partners directly from their corporate network. Before, this was only possible from stand-alone personal computers which were connected to the Internet. Significant savings are made possible by eliminating duplicated communication facilities and the reduction in telecommunication and business costs.

As with all DFTS services, there is a guarantee of continuous improvement to user services with no capital costs for the MoD to budget for. Strict defence guidelines apply. All accesses to Internet sources are recorded for audit purposes and additional monitoring devices, to screen e-mail from malicious software for example, add more protection. The 24-hour Help Desk is permanently on call to give assistance. The IGS was developed by Syntegra which is part of BT.

There is also a **Point to Point Service** for voice and data that integrates the existing networks, establishing guaranteed service levels and upgrading all equipment to a common advanced technology platform.

Finally there are a series **of Managed Services**. As part of the move to a new numbering system an MoD Centralised Operator Service was established. It operates from four principal Centres – Dumbarton, Kettering, Wakefield and St Helens. These Operator Assistance Centres offer a single point of contact for all internal and external enquiries.

Beginning in May 1998, a new Directory Enquiries Service was offered for all three armed services with a Directory database that is updated every day. Details of ships alongside will be on the database within 30 minutes. Perhaps inevitably, there have been problems with the common directory enquiries. Call Centres have needed to give civilian operators additional training in coping at speed with the military jargon and acronyms used so liberally. In the future it is likely that paper directories will be replaced by CD-ROMS, which can be updated and produced more quickly and economically.

The world of communications has never stood still. When carrying out their telecommunications study in 1992, the Ministry of Defence considered the implementation of a single fixed telecommunications system as the keystone for future communications strategy until the year 2010. Yet even within that ten year time frame, it was not possible to predict how quickly and how radically communications would develop at the end of the 20th Century. Even while the DFTS contract was running its course, the MoD began to negotiate terms to bring the telecommunications component of their Corporate Headquarters Office Technology System (CHOTS) within the system and this was completed on 16 March 2000. CHOTS now links the whole of the Department and provides transmissions up to SECRET security level. Mobile telecommunications is another field where growth has been so fast that the MoD are continually monitoring the impact it will have on their fixed telecommunications planning requirements.

The contract between the MoD and INCA is designed to ensure 'value for money', and year on year BT needs to remain commercially competitive. In 2007 it will be open to re-tender, and having invested so heavily in the integration and modernisation of the Services' Fixed Telecommunication System, INCA will want to see their contract renewed. It is technically feasible to allow continuous technological update, and there is now an Integrated Project Team (IPT) tasked to bridge the cultural differences between a commercial organisation and the military.

The IPT is yet another new concept to be introduced to the DFTS programme. IPTs were introduced by the MoD as a result of the Smart Procurement Initiative contained in the 1998 Strategic Defence Review. The submission of new communications ideas to the MoD is an ongoing process. As with most large-scale capital projects, it is a question of evolvement and improvement rather than replacement, although in some cases replacement may be required.

The contract also calls for BT to meet all operational requirements, and at the DFTS Network Control Centre, Basil Hill Barracks, Corsham, a Military Operations Manager sets the priorities. For example, BT were informed of the Sierra Leone operation, and what UK-based communications would be needed. In times of crisis, demands can be on an 'in minutes' basis, when DFTS personnel work round the clock to ensure targets are achieved.

Just as the GPO before them, BT will be able to make whatever additions and changes are needed to keep up with the constant technological changes ahead. DFTS takes the armed forces to the 21st Century and beyond. It will serve more than 200,000 users making 2.5 million calls a day across 2,445 sites in Britain. A modern digital-based telephone service links forces at the touch of a button, providing access to PC networking, e-mail, ISDN, videoconferencing, Intranet and internet, together with Wide Area and secure Local Area Networks. Voice and data applications beyond the imagination of the soldiers, sailors and airmen of 50 years ago have now been rolled out to defence users; the Private Sector and the Armed Services have worked together as partners and herald a new era in military communication.

The Last Word

The last commercial telegraph message to be sent from United States shores was tapped out in Morse Code in July 1999 from a coastal town just west of Silicon Valley. It was dispatched by Globe Wireless who said that e-mail, fax and radio messaging had ended the commercial viability of the telegraph.

The content of that final transmission was the same as the very first message which Samuel Morse had tapped out in 1844 and sent from Washington to Baltimore. It read "What hath God wrought?"

CHRONOLOGY OF THE DEVELOPMENT OF MILITARY COMMUNICATIONS

2nd Century BC
The Greeks devised a method of communication using torches

1st Century BC
The Persian King Darius set up a chain of soldiers on hilltops to shout messages to each other

1568
The approach of the Spanish Armada was signalled by a chain of beacons from the Westcountry to London

1684
Dr Robert Hook proposed a form of signalling using simple shapes hung in a wooden frame, forerunner of the shutter telegraph

1779
Vice Admiral Lord Shuldham established a signals code to be used from the Tower of Maker Church Plymouth

1792
Claude Chappe invented the Radiated Telegraph

1816
Admiral Sir Home Popham introduced the Sea Telegraph for mounting on ships

1821
Karl Dauss invented the Heliotrope, a more modern form of the Heliograph

1837
William Cook and Charles Wheatstone produced the first electric telegraph system in Britain

1855
Samuel Morse patented his Morse Code

1937
GPO Engineering Department becomes involved with the provision of landline communications to support the Filter Rooms and Chain Home radar network in support of UK air defence. This function continues to the end of the war

1940
Two Executive Engineers from GPO Research Department Dollis Hill design the first electro-mechanical BOMBARDIER (BOMBE) Computer for the decryption of German Enigma traffic at the Signal and Cipher School, Bletchley Park

1939–45
Many GPO Engineers seconded to Telecommunications Research Establishment (TRE) to work on radar and similar devices

1939–45
Whole of GPO Engineering Department committed to war work and the repair of the national communications infrastructure, especially repairs to telephone cables in dockyards, ports, on airfields, supply centres and government buildings

1945–1985
The Post Office Air Defence Group formed to provide specialist engineering support to the RAF for the design and installation of landline and ground to air communications at radar stations, airfields, command headquarters in the UK and abroad

1945–85
Design and installation of voice comms network to support the Royal Observer Corps and the UK Weapons Monitoring Organisations (UKWMO). This support continued until the ROC disbanded in the early nineties

1960–1973
Post Office Telecomms responsible for the design and installation of communications to support the RAF/National Air Traffic Control organisation (NATS) LINESMAN and MEDIATOR air traffic control (ATC) systems

1974–85
Post Office Telecomms responsible for the design and installation of on-base commu-

nications in support of the RAF's airfield survival measures (ASM) hardening programme for RAF Germany's four airfields and associated squadrons

1982–84
Post Office engineers responsible for the design of all fixed communications cabling
networks in the Falkland Islands Theatre of Operations, particularly the airfields at
RAF Stanley and Mount Pleasant and command and control centres

1985–93
BT awarded the contract for the design and installation of the Army's FASTNET
switched telephony and data network. Work completed in 1993

1986–90
BT awarded contract to design and install the Royal Navy's Naval Fixed Telecommunications System (NFTS), a voice and data network that inter-linked all naval
establishments and dockyards in the UK, based on System X technology. Completed
in 1990

1990–93
BT awarded contract to design and instal the RAF's Admin Network at all RAF stations in the UK

1989–90
Project for the design and installation of a System X based system to support voice and
data communications in MoD's Whitehall complex

1996
BT as leader of the INCA Consortium are awarded DFTS Contract – it is the largest
contract awarded to date under the PFI Initiative

APPENDIX TWO

DESCRIPTION OF A TELEPHONE 1877

To the Editor of the R.E. Journal from Lieutenant A W Bagnold, RE.

Sir,

Having been so fortunate as to have had lent to me a pair of telephones which 'spoke' remarkably clearly, and having found their construction so simple that I was enabled in a very short time to construct a pair for myself which answer very well, I send you sketches of the same hoping they may be of interest.

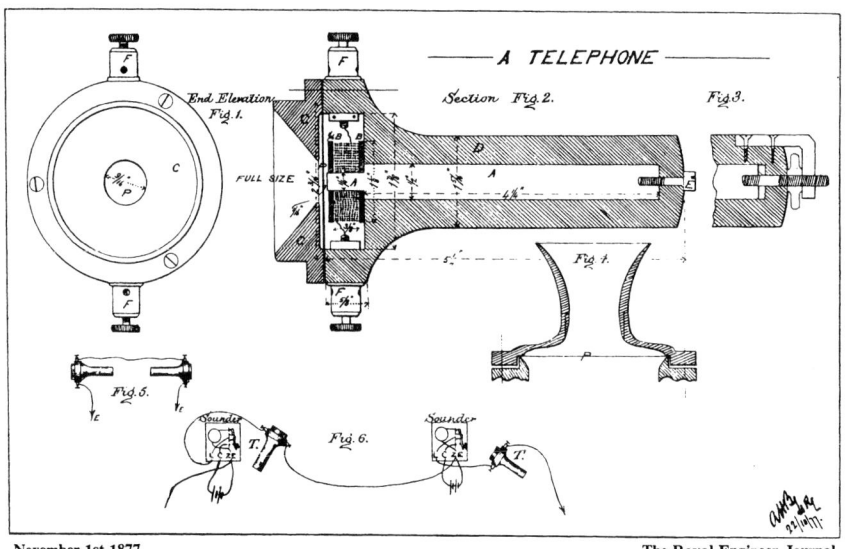

November 1st 1877   The Royal Engineer Journal

DESCRIPTION

Fig 1 is an end elevation of mouthpiece of and Fig.2 a section of a telephone.

AA is a round bar magnet held in a round wooden body D by a brass screw E.

The end of this bar magnet nearest to the mouthpiece is turned down to a smaller diameter (about quarter of an inch) and on to the pin thus formed are fixed (by friction only) two ebonite disks BB – the pin being turned slightly tapered to allow of these discs being jammed on tight.

Between these discs is wound on about 30 ohms of 38 gauge silk-covered wire. The ends of the coil are soldered to the brass terminals FF.

In front of the coil and at a distance from the end of the magnet of rather than less than one sixteenths of an inch, a circular plate of ferrotype iron P (the enamelled iron on which ferrotype photographs are taken) is fixed.

This plate is held in its place by being gripped between the body of the instrument and the wooden mouthpiece CC, which is fastened to the body by three or four screws as shown in Fig. 1.

To use the telephone, it is simply held in the hand and the mouth or ear is closely applied to the mouthpiece CC according as it is desired either to speak or to listen.

Fig 5 shows the ordinary method of "connecting up". The room in which a telephone is used must be kept very quiet as the sound emitted is somewhat faint though very distinct. The voices of particular individuals can be easily recognised and conversation carried on as easily as through a speaking tube.

The sounds of a piano are best transmitted by the telephone being held with its mouth against the sounding board. The sounds of a band are best transmitted when the telephone is suspended mouth downwards about a foot above the floor and in the centre of the circle of musicians. It is easier to hear a person speaking in low tones of voice than in high tones of voice.

The telephones work perfectly clearly through 36 miles of "C" Troop telegraph cable coiled up on the wagons and conversation can be carried on through 26,666 ohms of resistance in addition – representing in resistance about 1,100 miles of ordinary No. 11 B.W G. telegraph wire.

Fig. 3 represents a method of adjusting the distance of the magnet from the plate, that I would recommend to anyone undertaking the manufacture of a telephone.

Fig. 4 represents a form of mouth-piece I have tried of thin wood, in which the vibrating plate is gripped by its extreme edge only. No very decided advantage is, however, gained by this method of construction.

Fig. 6 represents a convenient way of connecting up with sounders in circuit for the purpose of being able to "call up" the distant station, as the sound emitted from a telephone is inaudible at a few inches from the instrument. Morse signals, from a voltaic battery, can be easily read by sound on a telephone.

A polarized F.S. Recorder placed in circuit seriously interferes with the action of the telephone. Morse signals made by moving the armature of a polarized Recorder placed in circuit are distinctly audible on the telephone. The dimensions given in the sketches give no peculiar advantages.

Ferrotype iron is not essentially necessary. Any thin iron plate will do. Thin tinned plate answers well.

The precise action of this instrument cannot be easily explained but the following gives it roughly. The Plate P takes up every vibration of the voice of the speaker and by its alternate approaches to and retrogressions from the end of the magnet, causes a series of disturbances in the distribution of its magnetism. These, according to well known laws of electro-dynamics, induce rapid electrical pulsations in the coil and line wire, which reciprocally affect the magnet at the distant station. Vibrations are thus produced in the plate at the distant station exactly similar to those imparted to the plate at the near station, although their amplitude is not so great. In this manner both the "pitch" and "timbre" of the voice are represented but not its volume. It is worthy of note that no effect is visible on a reflecting galvanometer placed in circuit when the telephones are being used.

How to increase the volume of the sound emitted from the telephone appears to be the great difficulty and on the successful solution of this problem would appear to depend the practical utility of the instrument.

I have etc

Arthur W. Bagnold Lieut. R.E.

Aldershot 22 October 1877

GLOSSARY

Name/Acronym	Meaning
2ATAF	2nd Allied Tactical Air Force (NATO)
AASF	Advanced Air Striking Force (RAF)
AFCENT	Allied Forces Central Europe
AER	Army Emergency Reserve
AFTA	Army Fixed Telecommunications Agency
AFS	Air Formation Signals; Independent Signals Units created between the Wars to meet RAF needs. 'Formation' became 'Support' in 1960s
Anthropo Day and Night	A portable telegraph invented by Knight Spencer in 1797
AOC-in-C	Air Officer Commander-in-Chief
ASM	Airfield Survival Measures
ATC	Air Traffic Control
ATN	Army Telephone Network
ATO	Authorised Telecommunications Officer
ATTA	Army Tactical Telecommunications Agency
BAFO	British Air Forces of Occupation
BEF	British Expeditionary Force
Bentley Priory	Headquarters of Fighter Command in World War Two, established 1936; all communications provided by GPO

B.F. Set	The 50-watt Trench Spark Set used in World War One needed three men to carry it and another three to handle the aerial gear and spare batteries
BOMBARDIER (BOMBE)	First electro-mechanical computer for decoding German ENIGMA signals at Bletchley Park
Bomber Broadcast	Communications network for Bomber Command
BOXER	RAF bespoke secure system which provides the Network to carry the UNITER Secure Telecommunications system
BRITCON	British Contingent of UNPROFOR in Bosnia
BRITMEDBAT	British Medical Battalion (part of UK contribution to UNPROFOR in Bosnia)
CCG	Control Commission Germany, set up after World War Two with representatives of British, French, US and USSR governments
C&R	Control and Reporting (radar)
CH	Chain Home – early warning radar stations
CHESHIRE	Operation CHESHIRE was the name given to RAF humanitarian flights into Sarajevo
Circuit Switching	A method of connecting voice and data Telecommunications. When a user makes a transmission a circuit is established in an exchange and this connects the user with the intended recipient for the duration of the transmission. The two users then have exclusive use of the circuit until the connection is released. Contrast with POINT-TO-POINT where permanent connections exist

CHOTS	Stands for Corporate Headquarters Office Technology System. RESTRICTED and SECRET electronic mail and office administration system for the MoD's administrative centre and some headquarters
COLOSSUS	The world's first electronic programmable computer, assembled at Bletchley Park in December 1943
COMBRITCON	Commander British contingent of UNPROFOR Bosnia
COMCAN	Commonwealth Communications Army Network
CPA	Communications Projects Agency (Royal School of Signals, Blandford, Dorset)
CSSAD	Committee for Scientific Survey of Air Defence
CIGS	Chief of the Imperial General Staff
DEW Line	Defence Early Warning Stations (American)
DCSA	Defence Communications Services Agency – The Executive Agency of the Ministry of Defence, set up to manage the Department's telecommunications. Their responsibility includes liaison with BT concerning performance of the Defence Fixed Telecommunications Service
DFTS	Defence Fixed Telecommunication Service
D Mark 3	Standard World War One army telephone
DTN	Defence Teleprinter Network, for communications needs of all three Services
EMD	Electromechanical Motor Driven

EMP	Electro Magnetic Pulse
ENIGMA	Developed by German inventor Dr Arthur Schervius in 1920s to encode documents for security. Taken up by German Navy in 1926, and German Army in 1928. Poland sent a machine to Britain following the outbreak of World War Two; it was decoded and the intelligence gained was codenamed ULTRA
ERT	Earth Return Telegraphy, which needed only one wire for telegraphic transmission
EUROMUX	Multiplex equipment carrying speech, facsimile and data communication to wherever needed
FAME	Frequency Assignment Management Equipment (system used during Gulf War)
FASTNET	Codename for the system which carried the Army Telephone Network (ATN)
FoS	Foreman of Signals
'Fruit Machines'	Calculators used in radar stations to convert range and bearing figures into map grid references on operator display panels
Fullerphone	Invented by Captain (later Major General) A C 'Boney' Fuller in 1915, it made buzzer signals secure
GCCS	Government Code and Cipher School, based at Bletchley Park
GCI	Ground Control of Interception
GEO orbit	Geostationary orbit (orbit of satellite operating without antennae)
GOR	Gun Operation Room. There were three of

	these at the Army HQ of 1st AA Signals in the disused Brompton Road London Underground Station during World War Two
GPO	General Post Office, later the Post Office Corporation
GPS	Global Positioning System
HCU	Heavy Conversion Unit
Heliograph	The use of reflected sunlight to flash messages. The first modern machine, with an oscillating mirror, was invented by Sir Henry Manse in 1869
Heliotrope	Invented by German Karl Dauss in 1821, this was a surveying instrument consisting of two mirrors at right angles used to measure a steady beam of light
HQ	Headquarters
INCA	A team led by BT combining the expertise of British Telecom, Lockheed Martin, GEC Marconi, GPT Strategic Communications and Syntegra, the software house of BT, chosen as prime contractor for DFTS
Intelsat	International Satellite Organisation, established 1964
LADA	London Air Defence Area
LAN Interconnect	Local Area Network Interconnect Service, a DFTS service helping the defence community to share and exchange computerised information
LEO	Low earth orbit (used by satellites)
LINESMAN	UK's Plan Ahead integrated air defence system

'Maggie'	A magnetic detector, used as a receiver, produced by Marconi in the early 20th Century
MEDIATOR	Air traffic control system
Mercury	Roman messenger of the gods (in Greek, Hermes), originally adopted as badge of Telegraph Battalion and still used by Royal Corps of Signals
MoD	Ministry of Defence
Morse Code	A system of substituting dots and dashes for letters, invented by Samuel Morse in 1832
NADGE	NATO Air Defence Ground Environment
NATO	North Atlantic Treaty Organisation, created 4 April 1949
NATS	National Air Traffic Control organisation
NFTS	Naval Fixed Telecommunications System (replaced Royal Navy's Telephone Network)
Operation SEALION	Hitler's invasion plan for Britain
ORANGE YEOMAN	British Army radar set
ORP	Operational Readiness Platform (RAF)
OTU	Operational Training Unit (RAF)
PABX	Private automatic branch exchanges
Packet Switching	A system which transmits data in 'packets' so allowing more efficient use of the network as paths in the network can be shared with other users. The data are broken up into small groups or Packets. There is no physical circuit but the data share a 'virtual circuit' with other users. It is only used for data transmissions in the Defence Fixed Telecommunications System

PFI	Private Finance Initiative
Point-to-Point System	Terminals are linked by permanent physical circuits. Less complex than circuit switched networks and quick in response time. But inefficient in resource use because lines still exist but lie dormant when not in use, rather than being formed for a particular communication as with circuit switching. May be used for voice and data transmission
P&T Group	Post & Telecommunications Group, afterwards TELS Group
POC	Post Office Communications (became British Telecommunications plc – BT – in 1983)
POLO	Post Office Liaison Officer
POR	Post Office Rifles, a volunteer corps formed in 1868
Post Office Air Defence Group	Provided specialist engineering support to RAF for their communications in the UK and abroad
PSS	Packet Switched Service (DFTS provides the UK defence community – including British Forces in Germany – with a single unified data network)
PTARMIGAN	Static communications system first operationally deployed during Gulf War
QRA	Quick Reaction Alert
RAAF	Royal Australian Air Force
Radiated Telegraph	Invented in 1792 by Frenchman Claude Chappe, it had pivoted arms to send signals along roads radiating from Paris. Variations included the Gamble machine of 1797 and the Paisley machine of 1811

RAuxAF	Royal Auxiliary Air Force
RAF	Royal Air Force, founded April 1918
RAFTN	RAF Telephone Network for administration across UK stations
RE	Royal Engineers
Reichspost	German Post Office prior to the formation of DBP Deutsche Bundespost
RISTACOM	Rationalisation of Inter Service Telecommunications Agreement made in late 1960s whereby the RAF assumed responsibility for long haul communications including SKYNET, and the Army for ground and static communications
RFC	Royal Flying Corps, formed in May 1912
ROC	Royal Observer Corps
ROTOR	UK plan to improve Cold War radar cover
RNAS	Royal Naval Air Service
SACEUR	Supreme Allied Commander Europe (NATO)
SCRA	Single Channel Radio Access System (Radio Trunk Extension of Ptarmigan)
Semaphore	Invented in 1801 by Frenchman Depillon, it had two pivoting arms mounted directly on a mast
Shutter Telegraph	Invented in 1796 by the Revd Lord George Murray, it used shutters and letters in a large frame
SKYNET	Name given to the family of British military satellites

Social Call Service	GPO scheme allowing servicemen to phone their families on military networks to avoid delays
STARRNET	Static Radio Relay Network system, providing secure speech for the BAOR in Germany
STD	Subscriber Trunk Dialling
TA	Territorial Army
2TAF	2nd Tactical Air Force (RAF)
TELS Division	Previously Telecommunications Group
Thermionic valves	Patented by John Flemming in 1905, they enabled wireless sets to operate on medium and short waves
TRE	Telecommunications Research Establishment
TSEP	Technical System Executive and Plans (Signals team carrying out frequency management for Ptarmigan during Gulf War)
TTS	Telecommunications Traffic Superintendent
UKADGE	United Kingdom Air Defence Ground Environment, part of NATO Air Defence System
UKWMO	UK Weapons Monitoring Organisation
ULTRA	Intelligence gained by decoding the German ENIGMA machine
UNITER	Codename for the switches within the UK RAF bespoke secure system, forming part of the Minimum Military Core
USAF	United States Air Force

GLOSSARY

USSR	Union of Soviet Socialist Republics
V-Force	Bomber Command's Vulcans, Victors & Valiants
VF	Voice Frequency
Wheatstone Automatic Telegraph	Used in Boer War for heavy traffic
WAN	Wide Area Network – data communications network which covers long distances, i.e. links between towns and Service sites
W/T	Wireless Telegraphy

PICTURE CREDITS

Key: AQA   Army Quarterly & Defence Journal Archive
     BT   British Telecom
     BTA   BT Archives
     IW   Ian White
     Online The magazine of BT Defence (DFTS)
     RSM   Royal Signals Museum
     SO   Subject's own

Foreword   Page vi, Peter Cochrane (SO).

Frontispiece   Greek soldiers using fire signals (RSM).

Chapter One   Page 11, North American Indians, Page 12, Maker Church (both AQA).

Chapter Two   Page 14, Murray's Shutter Telegraph, Page 15, Murray's Shutter Stations, Page 16, Military Anthropo Telegraph, Page 17, Gamble Radiated Telegraph, Page 19, Knight Spencer's Invention, Page 22, The Heliograph (all RSM).

Chapter Three   Page 23, Cable Wagons, Page 24, Cable ploughs (both RSM); Page 28, Queen Victoria (AQA); Page 30, Peter Archer Painting, Page 31, Letter from H R Forster, Page 32, Telegram from Sir Garnet Wolseley, Page 32, Illustration of signallers' Telegraph tent, Page 33, Tony Theobald's painting of Wheatstone Automatic Morse Telegraph (all RSM); Page 36, Marconi (AQA).

Chapter Four   Page 41, Gilbert Holiday's painting WW1 (RSM); Page 42, Telephone switchboard at Montreuil (BTA); Page 43, Trench dugout, Page 46, Artillery Signallers, Page 48, Scottish Signal Company RE (All RSM). Maps on Pages 50 and 51, Ian White; Page 54, Carrier Pigeon, Page 54, Dog carrying cable (both RSM).

PICTURE CREDITS

Chapter Five   Page 59, The Steel-Bartholomew Plan, Page 63, The Fifty-Two Squadron Scheme, Page 64, The Reorientation Scheme (all from *The Air Defence of Great Britain* by John Bushby); Page 66, Letter confirming Royal Warrant for the Corps of Signals (RSM).

Chapter Six   Page 70, Post Office Poster from *The Post Office Went to War* (BTA); Page 72, Maurice Le Marchant (SO); Page 73, Post Office Decontamination Squad and Searchlight Drill (BTA); Page 75, Bernard Brown (SO); Page 76, Basil Woods (SO); Page 77, Spitfire and Hurricane (AQA); Page 78, Map of Maritime defence (After B. Collier 1957); Page 81, Dowding letter (RSM); Page 83, Trafalgar Exchange 1944, Page 83, GPO Exchange HQ, St Martins-le-Grand, (both BTA); Page 86, Fred Nash (SO); Page 87, GPO Engineers repair damaged trunking (BTA); Page 88, Ron Pidgley (SO); Page 89, German artillery unit and ENIGMA machine (RSM); Page 90, Bletchley Park (AQA); Page 90, Dr Tommy Flowers, Page 91, COLOSSUS (Both BTA); Page 92, D-Day (AQA); Page 93, Peter Archer's painting ' Swiftly Ashore!, Page 94, Wireless Set No. 10, Page 95, Painting of Corporal Thomas Waters (all RSM); Page 97, HMTS *Monarch* (BTA); Page 99, Lancaster Bomber (AQA).

Chapter Seven   Page 100, Germany in 1945 (AQA); Page 101, Bill Findlay (SO); Page 103, Type 80 Radar (From *The Air Defence of Great Britain* by John Bushby); Page 104, Type 64 Radar console (RAF Museum, Neatishead); Page 104, Joseph Stalin (AQA); Page 108, A.J. Mashford (SO); Page 110, UK's first nuclear Weapon (AQA); Page 111, Avro Vulcan (RAF Museum, Hendon).

Chapter Eight   Page 113, P & T Group in Germany, Page 114, 1 (BR) Corps Switchboard (both BTA); Page 118, Wessex Helicopter (AQA); Page 123, GPO TELS Liaison Group (BTA); Page 124, Commonwealth Telecommunications Network (BT); Page 125, SKYNET 1 (AQA); Page 126, Ben Morgan OBE (SO).

Chapter Nine   Page 128, Map of Falkland Islands (Colonel James Sweetman); Page 129, HMS *Hermes*; Page 130, HMS *Fearless* (both AQA); Page 131, Peter Archer's painting of the landing at San Carlos, Page 132, Clansman radio (both RSM); Page 133, restoring Communications post Falklands Conflict, Page 134, Fully armed Phantom Aircraft on Stanley Airfield, Page 135, Triffid Radio equipment, Page 136, Post Office Liaison Officer Ian White, Page 141, San Carlos Water (all IW).

Chapter Ten   Page 142, Berlin Wall (AQA); Pages 143/4, INCA Graphic (Online); Page 148, MoD Main Building (AQA).

Chapter Eleven   Page 152, General Rupert Smith (AQA); Page 153, Soldier in The Gulf and Satellite Ground Station, Page 154, Ptarmigan, Page 155, TSEP Team and Ptarmigan, Page 158, Ptarmigan (All RSM); Page 160, Post 1980 Map of Balkan States, Page 162, British UN Soldiers in Bosnia, Page 163, Transportable Satellite Ground Terminals (all AQA); Page 165, Transportable Earth Station (TES) in Kosovo, Page 167, BT's TES in front of MoD's South Concourse (Ken Gerreli, BT).

Chapter Twelve   DFTS Contract, Page 170, INCA Graphic, Page 173, Huw Rees, Page 176, Network Management Control Centre and takeover of BOXER and UNITER networks, Page 179, the INCA team, Page 180, MoD Centralised Operator Services (all ONLINE).

ACKNOWLEDGEMENTS

We are grateful to many people throughout the United Kingdom, both from within the Armed Services and from the Civilian Sector, for providing help and information during the research and writing of this book.

BT is a large organisation, but we were especially involved with those at BT Defence who were universally helpful and encouraging. We especially wish to

Alan Jackman

acknowledge the encouragement and help provided by our mentor, Alan Jackman. He believed from the beginning in the book's concept, and was enthusiastic throughout our work. Without his support and direction, the book would not have been written.

Many current and past employees of BT gave us invaluable first-hand accounts of their experiences. Our thanks are due to Eric Moore and to Dick Durrant, Barry Bull, Sandy Hamilton and Kelvin Rawles of BT Government National Accounts (subsequently BT Defence) for their help in providing background information for Chapter Ten. David Spring talked to us about the part played by BT in providing fixed communications during the Falklands War, the Gulf War and for the Army Telephone Network. Ken Gerreli, International Systems Engineer with BT Defence, went to considerable trouble to provide us with detail about BT's welfare call service in Bosnia and BT's Transportable Earth Stations during the Kosovo conflict, which provided on the spot communication links between the Balkans and the Minstry of Defence.

The staff at BT Archives, too, in the old Holborn Telephone Echange, deserve acknowledgement. We would particularly like to thank Derek Reid for the enthusiastic help which he gave us in locating photographs showing the Post Office's involvement during World War Two. David Hay and Barbara Griffiths also gave help with our initial research.

Ben Morgan, OBE (former Head of TELS Division, 4 Signal Brigade in Germany), generously shared his experiences with TELS Group in Germany with us, providing many fascinating anecdotes about his involvement with the development of fixed communications in BAOR, and much background about the period immediately following World War Two.

The old members of the Post Office AD Group gave considerable assistance in describing the Group's involvement with air defence communications, both at home and in Germany. Tom Behan provided his insight into working with the V-Force, George Young and John Baxter gave us the description of the LINESMAN Network and Graham Saville provided much information about RAF Germany..

Personal reminiscences of their experiences in World War Two – featured in Chapter Six – came from former GPO personnel Bernard Brown, David Buckley, Bill Findlay, the late Maurice le Marchant, Arthur Mashford, Fred Nash and Ron Pidgley.

We also thank Major Craig Tilson who supplied the history of 81 Signals Squadron and 21 Signal Regiment which appear in Chapter Eight.

At the Royal Signals Museum, we would like to thank Tim Sankus (Archivist) and Roger Pickard (former Curator) for making their archives available to our staff for research, including all back copies of the *Journal of the Royal Signals*, copies of *Corps Life* and other archive material. We also wish to acknowledge their generosity in allowing us to use numerous photographs and images from the Museum displays and publications.

Wing Commander C G Jefford, MBE, BA of the Royal Air Force Historical Society provided information about the involvement of former GPO telephone engineers and telegraphists during World War Two at the two Schools of Wireless Telegraphy at Hamble and Prestwick. He also gave much useful background about the Bomber Boxes which the GPO provided and maintained. These were telephone landlines which allowed Bomber Command HQ to communicate directly with crews at cockpit readiness. They provided the main means of launching the dispersed V-Bomber Force from the 1960s onwards; the remnants of the system were still operational in the early 1980s.

For their help in providing information about the provision of the new fixed communications systems on the Falkland Islands after the conflict, we wish to thank WO2 FoS (Retd) David Bowers for the descriptions of the work he carried out with 21 Signal Regiment, and WO2 (Retd) Tom Hornby for his memories of the work which he and Ian White carried out on the design of cable works at RAF Stanley and RAF Mount Pleasant. Colonel (Retd) Bob Stark helped with his detailed description of the laying of two submarine cables and the planning of FITS. We are also grateful to Lieutenant Colonel (Retd) James Sweetman for permission to quote from his article for the Royal Signals Institution (RSI) on the design and implementation of the

FITS network and the laying of submarine cables, and for the map of the Falkland Islands on page 128. Air Marshal Sir Thomas Stonor, KBE, RAF (Retd) assisted with the runway lengths at RAF Stanley.

Former and present members of the Signals Regiment were equally helpful. Colonel (Retd) Roger Thompson, Commanding Officer 30 Signal Regiment during the Falklands War, Lieutenant Colonel Peter Barron, currently Bowman and Digitisation Military Team, and former Warrant Officer Yeoman of Signals and Captain (Retd) Tony Reynolds gave us military background about communications during the Falklands War. Colonel Barron was also helpful in giving general information about communications during the Gulf War, and Captain Steve Whytock, MBE gave us useful information about his role in setting up fixed communications in Bosnia.

We also wish to recognise the assistance of the Ministry of Defence, Air History Branch, which provided useful source material about RAF communications between the wars and landline communications pre-World War Two; the Public Record Office, Kew, for Operational Records of the Royal Air Force between World War One and World War Two; and the National Army Museum, where Sarah Jones provided help with the history of the Post Office Rifles.

Last but by no means least, we owe a great debt to Ian White, who helped throughout the period of our work, in suggesting paths of research, loaning reference books, assisting with photographs, reading chapter drafts as they were written, and providing invaluable information about the development of Radar, the V-Bomber Force, RAF Germany and Airfield Survival Measures. He also gave us a detailed account of his involvement in the construction of the new Fixed Telecommunications System in the Falkland Islands, which was incorporated in Chapter Nine. Ian retired from BT in the summer of 2000. He has now begun a new chapter in his life at Anglia Polytech University (APU), and is also working on his own book, provisionally entitled *Defending the Dark Sky – A History of UK Night Air Defence 1912-1942*.

BIBLIOGRAPHY

The Air Defence of Great Britain by John Bushby (Ian Allen)

Army Quarterly & Defence Journal January 1996, UK Military Telecommunications, by Alan Jackman, CEng, MIEE

The Battle of Britain by John P Milford Reid (1975)

Defending the Dark Sky by Ian White, IEng, AMRAeS (unpublished)

The Electron & Sea Power by Vice Admiral Sir Arthur Hezlet (Davies, 1975)

Falkland Islands War – A Signaller's Viewpoint by Lieutenant Colonel Roger Thompson, Major Keith Butler and Captain John Thomas, all Royal Signals

Historical Record of the London Regiment compiled by Colonel A R Martin (A R Martin, 1975)

The Journal of the Royal Signals Regiment Vol VII, Summer 1967, The Fullerphone

Ibid Vol XX, Summer 1991, Objective 2 and the Army Field Telecommunications Agency, by Colonel M C Spence

Ibid Vol XXI, Summer 1992, The Fixed Representative Communications System, by Captain M Ramshaw, Royal Signals

Ibid Vol XIX, Summer 1989, The Defence Communication Network, by Wing Commander P M Ford, RAF

Mr Barrow of the Admiralty by Christopher Lloyd (Collins, 1970)

The Old Telegraphs by Geoffrey Wilson (Phillimore, 1976)

Post Office Journal Victory Edition 1945

The Post Office Went To War by Ian Hay (HMSO 1946)

The Rifle Volunteers by Ray Westlake (Chippenham, 1982)

The Semaphore by T W Holmes (Stockwell, 1983)

The Swan (30 Signal Regiment News), No 27 'Victory South Atlantic' Edition

Terriers in the Trenches: The Post Office Rifles at War 1914-1918 by Charles Messenger (Picton Publishing 1982, in association with the Post Office and British Telecom)

The Vital Link – a History of Royal Signals 1945-1985 by Philip Warner (Leo Cooper, 1989)

INDEX